CORRECTING

AMERICA'S

SHAME

*The Failure
of Public Education*

CORRECTING AMERICA'S SHAME

*The Failure
of Public Education*

WRITTEN BY
STEVEN HARLEM, PhD

Indigo River Publishing

Indigo River Publishing
3 West Garden Street, Ste. 718
Pensacola, FL 32502
www.indigoriverpublishing.com

© 2021 by Steven Harlem
First edition, 2021
Printed in the United States of America

All rights reserved. No portion of this publication may be reproduced, stored in a retrieval system, or transmitted by any means—electronic, mechanical, photocopying, recording, or any other—except for brief quotations in printed reviews, without the prior written permission of the publisher.

The opinions expressed in our published works are those of the author(s) and do not reflect the opinions of Indigo River Publishing, LLC, or its editors.

Correcting America's Shame: The Failure of Public Education | Steven Harlem, PhD, author
ISBN: 978-1-950906-90-1 | LCCN: 2020922872

Edited by Earl Tillinghast and Regina Cornell
Cover and Interior design by Robin Vuchnich

Special discounts are available on quantity purchases by corporations, associations, and others.

For details, contact the publisher at the address above. Orders by US trade bookstores and wholesalers: please contact the publisher at the address above.

With Indigo River Publishing, you can always expect great books, strong voices, and meaningful messages. Most importantly, you'll always find . . . words worth reading.

CONTENTS

Epigraph   vii

Teach with a Guiding Classroom Philosophy   1

Our Educational Heritage and the Reality of Students' Lives   11

Using Life Experiences to Magnify Your Creative Talents   29

Creating Classroom Trust and Confidence: A Blueprint for Achievement   43

The Rewards That Honor a Job Well Done   83

Thoughts on Reconstructing Our Educational System   101

Appendix: Attention Training Manual   123

References   128

Recommended Readings   132

Acknowledgments   133

Dedicated to the untold number of black and underprivileged individuals who have suffered the consequences from the prolonged failure of public education. Their unspoken goal, perpetuated by the illusion of their schooling, was simply to be a man in the family of men, bound by ties to other men. Educational inequities precluded this and divided them into separate ineluctable strata.
Their lives bear witness to the truth that only a principled education can remove the fetters of the past.

Epigraph

Between the man and the woman a child had hollowed himself out a place and fallen asleep. He turned in his slumber, and in the dim lamplight I saw his face. What an adorable face! A golden fruit had been born of these two peasants. . . .

I bent over the smooth brow, over those mildly pouting lips, and I said to myself: This is a musician's face. This is the child Mozart. This is a life full of beautiful promise. Little princes in legends are not different from this. Protected, sheltered, cultivated, what could not this child become?

When by mutation a new rose is born in the garden, all the gardeners rejoice. They isolate the rose, tend it, foster it. But there is no gardener for men. This little Mozart will be shaped like the rest by the common stamping machine. . . . This little Mozart is condemned. I went back to my sleeping car. I said to myself: Their fate causes these people no suffering. It is not an impulse to charity that has upset me like this. I am not weeping over an eternally open wound. Those who carry the wound do not feel it. It is the human race and not the individual that is . . . outraged here. I do not believe in pity. What torments me tonight is the gardener's point of view. . . . What torments is not the humps nor the hollows nor the ugliness. It is the sight, a little bit in all these men, of Mozart murdered.

—*Wind, Sand, and Stars*, Antoine de Saint-Exupéry

1

TEACH WITH A GUIDING CLASSROOM PHILOSOPHY

As I thought about how to introduce the events set forth in this book, I realized I was writing an adventure story. What is an adventure if it is not breaking new ground? An adventure is not necessarily physical; it is something that must touch us through the mind and heart. My hope is that the reader will now share this adventure with me and become an inspired and effective educator who contributes to the building of the world through the development of his or her own exceptional teaching innovations.

But first, imagine you are a historian and have been asked what you consider to be the most significant event(s) impacting the future of our country. Would it be global warming, terrorism, mass shootings, or other manifestations of social deviance? Although these events are obviously quite consequential, I believe the foremost problem our nation faces is the present failures of public education. This is particularly true when it comes to students of color and those from low-income backgrounds. The sooner that America acts, the better prepared the entire nation will be for the future.

It is painful to observe that at this point in our history, when we have the understanding and material resources to do almost anything we can imagine, we are still denying a large percentage of our society the knowledge, skills, and opportunity to have an equal chance to be satisfied with their contributions to life. Again, this is especially true for students of color and the underprivileged. This book is about the crass indifference to educating the underclasses leading to increased poverty, despair, helplessness, violence, and a plethora of social ills. How can we expect an individual to value the life of another if he does not value his own existence? This is not to ignore or fail to recognize the many sincere efforts scattered throughout our country that offer educational and vocational opportunities for the underprivileged. Mr. Ray Dalio, for example, the founder of the hedge fund Bridgewater Associates, gave millions for public education in the state of Connecticut. However, there is presently no national policy or even discussion during the pending 2020 presidential election to address the national public education crisis. Political quietism characterizes the prevailing norm. Money alone in this new century is not an answer and, now as in the past, will never solve this exigency. I believe we need a revolution in our public education system, not simply through the cybernation of knowledge, but one that results in an educational system that communicates a sincere belief in man's potential and the cultivation of an enhanced self-image in each and every individual child.

Chapter 2 will present some of the historical, time-honored goals and beliefs that helped establish the foundation of public education in our country. John Adams, our second president, wrote, "The education here intended is not merely that of the children of the rich and noble, but of every rank and class of people, down to the lowest and poorest."

Our nation was founded on the proposition "that all men are created equal." Unfortunately, there has been a deliberate erosion of these past values, leading to the present state of public education in our nation. Our educational problems did not begin with this present administration. For years politicians have simply thrown money at the crisis in public education without honest, comprehensive reform. This predicament was heightened with the appointment of billionaire heiress Betsy DeVos, an outspoken critic of government spending on public education, as Secretary of Education. Her selection influenced Dan Currell to write in the *National Review* in 2017, "We have the worst public schools in the developed world. In 1,200 American high schools, a third or more of the students do not graduate."

Can we ever determine one's ability without providing opportunity?

I hope the following chapters make a reasonable contribution to the remediation of this terrible injustice with its frightening consequences for the individual and society. To do less is cruel and indicative of an inequality that can only be considered deliberate.

Educator, writer, and activist Jonathan Kozol describes the disparities in public education as the restoration of America's apartheid. He also points out that we put more money into prisons than into schools, while black children in crowded schools are more segregated and their health and nutrition are poorer than their white counterparts'. He describes this situation as a nation bent on suicide.[1] The final chapter of this book will offer multiple broad-based educational solutions to reduce and, where possible, eliminate these inequalities.

As I write this chapter, my neighbor's son has been in India for two months recruiting employees to work in information technology and internet protocol telephony. He is unable to find enough qualified high school and college graduates for these positions in the United States. Cheaper labor, yes, but not the skills paired with the necessary and valued work ethic—values that should be part of our instructional agenda. Biology gives us a brain. A conscientious education turns it into a mind.

All teachers bring a philosophy into their classroom when they begin their careers. Their beliefs guide the ways they want to teach and a portion of their classroom goals. I was no different in this respect. My thoughts about what I considered to be beneficial in education and how teachers might best instill this began to form in high school. I attended a university-preparatory high school, where I experienced four unhappy years. Perhaps much of this was due to my own immaturity and youthful sensitivity. However, I felt most of my teachers at that time were oblivious and indifferent to the needs of adolescents. After graduation, I wanted no part of additional education.

Eight years later, feeling somewhat more mature, I entered college. Four years of class coupled with life experiences added to an already evolving educational philosophy and my approach to teaching. Eventually, as a teaching fellow, I obtained my PhD in psychology and functioned as a clinical/neuropsychologist until my recent retirement. During my career, I was fortunate to have taught in the Philadelphia public schools and both undergraduate and graduate students from multiple disciplines as well as medical residents. I continue to love teaching, especially to those who are underserved within our public schools. Ten years of undergraduate and graduate studies in addition to my teaching experiences reinforced my beliefs and developed the educational approaches now presented in this book. It is somewhat poignant to reflect that during my ten years at two universities, I can count on one hand those teachers who had a profound effect on my life. Those few teachers I still remember with appreciation for the way they encouraged and challenged my thinking while infusing my life with an authentic warmth presented with an honesty and patience borne of a wisdom I had yet to achieve.

The adventure I previously referred to and will present in detail in chapter 4 occurred when I, a Caucasian, taught English to predominately black and brown vocational high school students considered to be and treated as failures. Realizing how beaten down these young men and women were by failing grades and the terrible communication of how little or nothing could be expected from them, I knew that in some manner I was obligated to try to make them understand that for all of us, "the child is father of the man." Also, to ask them to consider this notion: Not "What do you want to be?" but rather "How do you want to be?" This thought was obviously alien in their school experience and, I suspect, still is not appreciated within our public education system.

I immediately scrapped the assigned standard curriculum and developed and implemented my own, making it relevant to their lives and emotional needs. I began to teach with the emphasis on valuing one's self and to stress the need to believe in their own self-worth. Learning and performance had become extremely difficult for these teenagers because it had become associated with competition and failure. Most were convinced they simply could not compete. While some aggression and defiant behavior was initially present, these behaviors disappeared as trust in me along with a belief in themselves evolved concurrent with their classroom successes. Ultimately, the majority of my students demonstrated a creativity that brought to each of them a sense of accomplishment they had not previously experienced. Their creative efforts were most impressive and were ultimately recognized at the local and national levels in the press and on radio and television.

I learned that, while rules and consequences are often inevitable, we cannot always improve learning by requiring teachers to follow scripted curricula tied to standardized tests in order to evaluate students' achievement. Rules and incentives will not provide teachers with the affective skills necessary to be an effective teacher. Even worse, I have witnessed how rules and incentives can destroy both the skill and the will critical to a truly effective education. The student is not a bench-bound learner. This view will negate the process of self-discovery and inhibit the potential for creativity.

I learned it may be easier to cram Shakespeare into students than to create a Shakespeare. The understanding and appreciation of this is precisely the goal of this book. Its realization will require dramatic changes in teacher selection and training along with providing relevant educational opportunities for pupils starting from infancy and continuing throughout their educational career. All teaching must take place in an atmosphere of acknowledgment and respect for the student's economic and social life. When the "system" gets in the way of the student's development, the system must yield and not the creative teacher whose style conflicts with the system. Hopefully, the reader will find guiding principles that will made his or her classroom labors infinitely more rewarding for the teacher and students alike. However, successful instruction first begins by a nonjudgmental acceptance of the lives of each individual pupil.

In 1884 the Austrian writer, philosopher, physician and social critic Max Nordau cautioned us that the moral pathology of civilization is in large part due to the whole organization of society rendering education inaccessible to those without means. It is incredible that many of our educators and government officials refuse to recognize that the abuse of students through neglect of their education will come back to hurt all of us by eroding the fabric of our civilized community. Do we not in some small manner have an obligation to ameliorate the myriad of personal and social ills associated with a preordained unequal opportunity? To do less is to contribute to the fallowing of our civilization.

Today, there is much discussion about how the changing technology, such as robotics, will force people out of work. While this is true, the greater truth is that a healthy social system always reaches a new equilibrium. When steam-powered iron ships caused the demise of the famed sailing vessels it eliminated the need for sail makers, wooden ship builders, et cetera, but our country adjusted and maintained its stability. Changing technology has always been a trade-off; of something old for something new. That society will adjust must be viewed in this context. However, this is where education plays a major role. Educational opportunities for all keep our society vital, not just by preparing individuals for specific changes but by providing them with the self-confidence and a broad range of adaptive traits to adjust to the inevitability of change that has always characterized our world.

This book is for everyone who is upset by and interested in correcting the unfairness; the unmerited misery stemming from unequal educational opportunities and the resultant personal and social consequences. I am aware that education presents some ethical difficulties as a true education should increase differences. If someone is good at something, should we not try to develop his or her own abilities? Thus, in some respects, education increases inequalities. While this may be necessary because of the complexities of our world, there are essential verities that serve as the foundation for all of us, and these truths are essential to success in the classroom and in life. However, to succeed we need tools that guide and direct our classroom efforts and strategies. The most important tool is in you—your values, beliefs, and determination to follow those principles you have developed.

COVID-19 has changed the traditional classroom model of teaching, and some of these changes may be permanent. Technology will support many of these changes, but ultimately, I believe, we will return to the time-honored model of classroom instruction.

While I do not use the mantra "Black Lives Matter," this is a theme inherent in this book that I hope is readily apparent.

The following paragraphs reflect my beliefs, those truths that determined what I brought to my classroom and influenced my interactions with my students. This not only guided my approach to teaching but is a reflection of how passionate I feel about the need for teachers to develop values that guide their interactions in this awesome responsibility, teaching.

It is as if I were thirteen again and back at school. My history book lies open, and I stare through the window at the clouds. How I despise this unbearable torture and wish that by some magic I could skip the remaining ten or so years and become a grown-up man.

Years later I realized that what I hated was that school lacked the completeness of life. It was a place for giving special lessons whose worth could only be understood by adults. A monastic factory designed to grind out uniform results, ignoring and punishing the individual, denying sensitivities, while it finished preparing one for life. But education is not preparation for life; it is life.

A true education must develop the emotions as well as the intellect. It should embrace the unique, the sensitive, the curious, while feeding the child's hunger for life. Freedom and spontaneity should prevail in an atmosphere of acceptance, which is related to the social and economic life of the student, not adherence to routine.

School is a spiritual adventure, a pilgrimage, where we should learn there are veritable problems of human relations. History taught by parroted references and literature stripped of its true meaning may blind us to the fact that the happiness we all seek can only be found in the warmth of human relations, and these relations must be created. Our problems are built in relation to others, and when troubled only a comrade can touch our hand and pull us free. When races come together there must be a bond of relation, or else we only have a collection of people that ultimately must collide.

Another lesson of life is that we are constantly challenged by life itself. Schools must help us face life—not by pointing out the bravery of Columbus or the tenacity of George Washington, but by teaching that a man's greatness, his courage, lies in his honesty and in his sense of responsibility. To be a man is precisely to be responsible. It is to feel shame at the sight of needless suffering, to take pride and feel that one is contributing to the building of the world whether by discovering a continent or by making a pair of shoes. These lessons add to the completeness of our lives.

Man's search for individual freedom should begin in school, where he is now least free, not because of disciplinary restraints but because a student cannot commit himself to work that lacks meaning. A person is only free when he is committed to something and that something holds meaning.

Another purpose of education is to teach the truth: that there are as many truths as there are men. Men are not separated by their truths but by their passions with which they embrace their truths. These are lessons that should be learned in school if education is to bear any relation to life. To teach less is criminal.

The teacher new to this challenge must keep in mind that four hundred years of persecution must leave their marks of suspicion and defensive hostility. Certainly not in all students, but a persecuted minority has good excuses for repaying hostility and contempt in the same coin. This may be difficult to deal with, but do not be put off by this as you are guided by those values and beliefs that reflect who you are and determine your behavior. The next chapter may help one better understand the source of enmity.

2

OUR EDUCATIONAL HERITAGE AND THE REALITY OF STUDENTS' LIVES

IT IS A TRUISM THAT TO UNDERSTAND the future it helps to have knowledge of the past. However, this bromide does not illuminate our present reality.

Historically, we are the recipients of constantly evolving educational philosophies and approaches. Most theories have their day and then fade because they are replaced, but if we look, the seeds of truth were planted and nourished over the centuries. As we review the fruits of these ideas, we unfortunately discern that over time many educational goals have been deliberately neglected except for particular classes of our society. To better appreciate this, a review of these historical ideals is considered appropriate to apprehend the degree of America's shame. The neglect of valued ideals should offend us all as it has caused untold amounts of unmerited misery and has ultimately been responsible for the destruction of lives. Thankfully, many of these very early educational ideas, like tentacles, have threaded their way through history and left their mark, serving as not only past but present teaching blueprints for us to use if we elect to do so. It is up to you, the reader, to rediscover these past values and reinterpret them in the light of the present.

Ever since Plato, and no doubt long before, knowledge has been held in high regard. Aristotle believed that our fundamental social practices constantly demanded choices—when to be loyal, how to be fair or confront a risk, or when and how to be angry. Making the right choices and acting rightly, in these circumstances, was not theoretical but practical and depended on one's ability to perceive the situation, have the appropriate feelings, and deliberate about what was proper in the circumstances and then act. This meant acting socially appropriately—being a good friend, parent, doctor, soldier, citizen, or statesman. It implied having the ability to figure out the right way to do the correct thing in a circumstance, with a particular person at a particular time. Aristotle stressed that rules and incentives were not enough to solve the problems we might face. He called this wisdom, *practical wisdom*. Wisdom must be practical because we all face these common issues. He stressed that practical wisdom must be cultivated by major institutions and urged the citizens and statesmen of the Athenian city-state to build institutions that encouraged citizens to learn to be practically wise.[2]

One has to question, at this point, Are our present institutions discouraging the teaching of the wisdom we need to succeed in our daily life and work? If so, what can be done to make up this omission? It is no accident that our lives are structured by administrative, bureaucratic, and moral rules that tell us how to relate and act in our complex society. We can never legislate morality, and the founders of our constitution well understood they could not depend on the goodness or wisdom of men. That is why John Adams in 1780 argued for "a government of laws and not of men." Wise laws, with constitutional checks and balances, would minimize the need for wise men. It is therefore no accident that we believe can get better outcomes by requiring teachers to follow scripted curricula tied to standardized tests and by punishing or rewarding students for their performances. At the same time, rules without wisdom are self-defeating and at best guarantee mediocrity. Sometimes, we are obligated to avoid following this practice and to

Aristotle's point: to do our work and lead our lives well, we need to know when and how to bend the rule.[2]

One cannot overstate the passion for knowledge in the ancient world. However, centuries of religious pluralism under paganism—three faiths living side by side in a mixed rivalry—sounded the death knell for this enthusiasm. The process began when Constantine made Christianity Rome's official religion, and this created the environment for the eventual fall of the Roman Empire, moving the known world into a time that would be described as the Dark Ages.[3]

Before moving on, I would be remiss if I did not mention the most influential thinker produced by Rome, Quintilian. Quintilian believed that educational training could not begin too soon; it started from the cradle, and this meant that careful thought must be expended upon the choice of the infant's nurses, whose speech served as a model for imitation. He felt the child's parents also carried a grave responsibility and should exercise the greatest care in the upbringing of their children.

While Greek and Latin were the languages of the day, Quintilian believed that language education should begin early but in a way that did not cause a child to dislike his or her studies. He felt the first instruction should be in the form of play, letting the pupil be asked questions and praised for his answers.

Quintilian stressed the goal of building a firm foundation in the elementary stages. Many wealthy Roman parents at that time preferred to engage a tutor for their children rather than to send them to school, believing that schools (as did Locke and Rousseau) had a demoralizing effect and corrupted the morals of many youngsters. Quintilian decided in favor of the school, stating, "The school is a society in miniature, and when the pupil becomes a member of the school community, he experiences, with a supportive teacher, the bracing influence of healthy competition." He added, "A skilled teacher can handle his class as a group and at the same time give individual attention to those who need it."

Quintilian was able to consider the process of education from the child's point of view. The teacher should remember that each pupil has his own individual characteristics and should be dealt along lines best suited to him. Quintilian felt strongly that the average pupil is not averse to learning; in fact, he delights in acquiring knowledge and really wants to make progress. If this quality appears to be lacking, more often than not, the fault is the teacher's and not the child's: "For there is absolutely no foundation for the complaint that but few men have the power to take in knowledge that is imparted to them, and that the majority are so slow of understanding that education is a waste of time and labor. On the contrary, you will find that most are quick to reason and ready to learn. Reasoning comes as naturally to man as flying to birds, speed to horses and ferocity to beasts of prey; our minds are endowed by nature with such activity and sagacity that the soul is believed to be produced from heaven."

Quintilian was adamantly opposed to corporal punishment, stating, "If you coerce the child when he is young by means of blows, what will you do when he is a young man who cannot be compelled through fear and still has many more important things to learn?" Quintilian described a good teacher of rhetoric as one who, above all, adopts the attitude of a parent and is cognizant that he is taking the place of those who entrust their children to him. While never losing his temper, the teacher will not ignore faults which deserve correction but in neither an abusive nor harsh manner. Quintilian insisted upon the friendly, sympathetic, and respectful relationship that ought to exist between teacher and pupils. His works were essentially lost until the fifteenth century, when they were rediscovered and then had a striking influence upon Renaissance thinkers, continuing even to the eighteenth century and, as you might infer, to some extent the present.[4]

Briefly, St. Augustine, who is best known as a theologian and philosopher, was also one of the great educational thinkers between the fourth and fifth centuries. He made it clear that the pupil does not necessarily take for granted what has been told to him by his teacher. The student is free to think about the conclusions reached by the teacher and decide that he does not accept them. The ancient Greek and Roman civilizations, as we have seen, significantly influenced pedagogy.

Historically, some scholars perceive Europe as having been plunged into darkness when the Roman Empire fell in 500 AD. During this time, feudalism was the dominant political system. Because the feudal system of labor hindered the possibility of upward social mobility, the poor had minimal opportunity to improve their condition. Religious superstition permeated the Catholic Church that often opposed the scientific advancements the Greeks and Romans had pioneered. Famine and disease were common. Bubonic plague—the Black Death—devastated Europe in the late 1340s and early 1350s, killing an estimated 100 to 200 million people. In addition, fighting between Europeans and Muslims of the Arab world during the Crusades that began in 1095 and ended in 1291 added to the number of deaths. This period, often described as a backward time in human history, came to an end around 1500 AD, as the Italian Renaissance and the Age of Discovery dawned. It is fair, however, to point out that the accomplishments of the Middle Ages came to be better understood in the eighteenth and nineteenth centuries. Some scholars limit and possibly reject the term Dark Ages as misleading.

By the dawn of the sixteenth century there was a greater appreciation of Greek writing throughout Europe. This engendered a new humanistic philosophy in students. It elevated to respectability the study of the physical and factual world and encouraged travel in search of new culture and knowledge. The number of educators and their ideas is staggering and well beyond the scope of this book. Therefore, I limited my review to those few educators I felt are most relevant to the objectives of this chapter so that those who aspire to be the best of the best in the classroom know they are supported and even guided by so many from the past.

A German in the seventeenth century by the name of Comenius did much in England as well as his own country to influence educators and school programs. He stressed the need for regularity in eating, sleeping, and daily exercise. He demanded safe places where children might run about. His emphasis of the need for guardians of health, nurses and baby carriers, found its expression in the modern nursery and nursery school. His argument that parents should be vitally concerned with all aspects of the child's development remains a crucial aspect of our present concerns.

Comenius understood that children are willing to learn if they see the immediate use or purpose, and if they are taught things they can understand in an interesting way. Tasks should be graded in difficulty and should involve learning through the senses in the first place. Lessons should be few and adjusted to the capacities of the pupils, who should not be required to memorize more than a few very important things. Punishment for bad work should be avoided, for it is the teacher's fault if a child does not learn. Since children learn through all their senses, not their ears alone, teachers must use drawings, pictures, wall writings, and other aids while encouraging pupils to write down their own records. The classroom should be light, clean, and pleasant, and the teacher kind and encouraging. In order to foster a sense of security and ensure smooth progress, methods should be consistent throughout the school. It must be appreciated that these insights were initially written four centuries earlier.

While today's notion of child development would not support Rousseau's eighteenth-century theories, he was a pioneer at that time in France, challenging the majority of thinkers who explicitly or implicitly subscribed to the doctrine of original sin. Rousseau took an entirely opposite point of view, stating, "Let us lay it down as an incontrovertible rule that the first impulses of nature are always right; there is no original sin in the human heart, the how and why of the entrance of every vice can be traced."[4]

An overview of the work of Pestalozzi is considered worthwhile as he, in the nineteenth century, continued to advocate for quality education for the masses. In Switzerland, he believed the education, while elevating and inspiring, lacked the solid and sufficient training of practical ability. He saw education as fitting the individual for his place in society. He stressed equal opportunity in education, stating it was the duty of society to develop each man's abilities to the fullest, and this could only be accomplished by providing good schools, high moral standards, and sound teaching methods. Education would prepare the individual for his future place in life, not in the sense of class distinction, but that he should be able to find satisfaction in his occupation and in his domestic life. Education should begin in childhood for all classes so they might obtain useful knowledge and development of the intellect along with moral and physical strengths. While reading, writing, and arithmetic were taught, they were considered subsidiary activities: "It is well done to make a child read and write, and learn to repeat—but it is still better to make a child think."[4] Pestalozzi's beliefs led to education becoming democratic; in Europe, education became available for everyone.

John Dewey is one of the giants in the history of educational theory. He argued that for education to become most effective, children should be given learning opportunities that enable them to link present content to previous experience and knowledge. He felt there was a need for learners to engage directly with their environment, in what came to be known as *experiential learning*, where knowledge comes from the impressions made upon us by natural objects. This approach also led to problem-based and inquiry-based learning. These were radical ideas at the turn of the twentieth century in America. Ultimately, he believed in a more balanced approach to education, in which teacher, students, and content were given equal importance in the learning process. Teachers then would facilitate and guide, thus giving students opportunities to discover for themselves and to develop as active, independent learners.[5]

My apologies again for not mentioning the dozens of educational thinkers, past and present, who have contributed to the educational/learning process. I should, however, like to briefly mention one more giant, a savant from India, Rabindranath Tagore. I first became attracted to his philosophy when he wrote, "The best textbook for the pupil is the teacher." In his educational curriculum, he advocated a teaching system that analyzed history and culture for the progress that had been made in breaking down social and religious barriers. This approach emphasized the ideas and innovations that had been made in integrating individuals of diverse backgrounds into a larger framework and in devising economic policies that emphasized social justice and narrowed the gap between the rich and poor. Tagore fought for a world where multiple voices were encouraged to interact with one another and reconcile differences within an overriding commitment to peace and mutual connectedness. He provided a model for the way multiculturalism can exist within a single personality, and the type of person which the educational process should be aspiring toward.[6]

It is impossible to succinctly summarize the contribution of all these educational theorists. One thing they all share is the belief that without a proper education, man cannot succeed and take his rightful place in society. There is an evolving awareness that the state would be well served if there was a quality education for its citizens and of how best to provide this education. For the Greeks and Romans, this education did not include all classes of citizens. The Age of Discovery brought with it not only an expansion of pedagogical ideas but also stressed the conviction that the nation would be better off if equal educational opportunities were made available to all its citizens whether they be rich or poor. As we think about the above theories and goals of education, there is also a core belief. And that is, all of instruction doesn't matter a bit if your students are not valued as being worthwhile.

While these democratic ideals offered us a rich heritage to build upon, the reality was different. On June 11, 1963, President John F. Kennedy addressed the nation: "The Negro baby born in America today, regardless of the section of the nation in which he is born, has about one-half as much chance of completing a high school as a white baby born in the same place on the same day, one-third as much chance of completing college, one-third as much chance of becoming a professional man, twice as much chance of becoming unemployed, about one-seventh as much chance of earning ten thousand dollars a year, a life expectancy which is seven years shorter, and the prospects of earning only half as much."

Despite President Kennedy's admonition, forty-three years later, the current status of education for students of color and the impoverished led Jonathan Kozol to assert there is "the restoration of apartheid schooling in America."[1] This clarion call has yet to be heeded. We must take an in-depth look at the present reality, causes, and consequences of unequal educational opportunities for students of color and the underprivileged if we are ever to make long-overdue changes.

Adding to the discriminatory practices, the Great Recession of 2007 to 2009 produced radical changes in the US economy. Poverty rates rose from 33 million in 2005 to more than 48 million in 2012. Less advantaged groups, including low-SES individuals and minorities, experienced the largest percentage of decline in wealth following this recession. National studies repeatedly show that less-educated adults experienced more economic hardships and had more difficulty recovering from the recession than those higher-educated adults. Since the 1970s, income inequality in the United States has increased, making the United States notably more unequal today than Europe. Research data reflects that the top 20 percent of income earners have privileged access to better educations, jobs, and wealth as well as a greater likelihood of stable marriages and neighborhoods and heathier lifestyles. Recent economic evidence indicates that socioeconomic inequality, in part related to subpar education, is a striking problem in contemporary America.[7] Knowing this, one must then look to the government to correct an untenable situation.

Ideally, public education should be apolitical, but history has proven otherwise. And too often, aside from providing funds, our government has given lip service to educational reform. Renovations in education would be better served by experienced and committed educators and not politicians. Like many politicians before him, President Donald

Trump has reduced investments in government-funded programs, like welfare, Social Security, and education. His initial budget featured a $9.2 billion (or 13 percent) reduction in federal spending for public education.

As previously mentioned, he appointed the billionaire heiress Betsy DeVos to serve as the Secretary of Education. She is an outspoken critic of government spending on social welfare and the public school system. One of her first acts as education secretary was to retract protections allowing transgender students to use bathrooms that correspond to their gender identity. She supported Trump's initial budget reduction of $9 billion in cuts to education, including after-school programs, career and technical education, and programs to hire and train teachers. In addition, she has promoted the privatization of public schools through vouchers and rolled back protections for vulnerable children.[8]

Beyond the specifics of reform legislation of education financing, the effectiveness of any nation's education system is also dependent on the success of the student population. To illustrate this, education in Finland is often cited because Finnish students consistently exhibit higher academic achievement than students in the United States. It must be pointed out, however, that Finland is a country of five and a half million people compared to the United States of over 330 million with over 50 million students in public schools. We do have unique educational problems. Despite our obvious complexities, we still should be able to glean some valued insights and goals to guide us from Finland's educational paradigm. In comparison to the US educational system, Finnish education is more personalized and less focused on quantitative achievement in key subjects. There are no mandated standardized tests in Finland, apart from one exam at the end of the students' senior year in high school. There are no rankings, no comparisons or competition between students, schools, or regions. Finland's schools are publicly funded. The people in the government agencies running them, from national officials to local authorities, are educators, not business people or career politicians. Every school has the same national goals and draws from the same pool of university-trained educators. The result is that a Finnish child has an excellent chance at getting the same quality education no matter if he or she resides in a rural village or a university town. *Equality* is the most important word in Finnish education.

Teachers in Finland spend fewer hours at school each day and less time in classrooms than American teachers. They use the extra time to build curricula and assess their students. Children spend far more time playing outside, and homework is minimal. Compulsory schooling does not begin until age seven, as they feel children learn best when they are ready.

It is almost unheard of for a child to show up hungry or homeless. Finland provides three years of maternity leave and subsidized day care to parents. Preschool is available for all five-year-olds with an emphasis on play and socializing. In addition, the state subsidizes parents, paying them around 150 euros per month for every child until he or she turns seventeen. Ninety-seven percent of six-year olds attend public preschool, where children begin some academics. Schools provide food, medical care, counseling, and, if needed, taxi service. Student health care is free.

Not until sixth grade will kids have the option to sit for a district-wide exam, and then only if the classroom teacher agrees to participate. While most do, results are not publicized. This is in marked contrast to the United States' fascination with standardized tests.

The school receives 47,000 euros a year to hire aides and special-education teachers, who are paid slightly higher salaries than classroom teachers because of their required sixth year of university training and the demand of their jobs. In 1979 the state required that every teacher earn a fifth-year master's degree in theory and practice at one of eight universities—at state expense. *From then on, teachers were effectively granted equal status with doctors and lawyers.* Quality applicants began flooding teaching programs, not because salaries were so high, but because autonomy and respect made teaching attractive.

All children, clever or less so, are taught in the same classrooms, with lots of special help available to make sure no child will be left behind. Even many of the most severely disabled can find a place in Finland's expanded vocational high schools, which are attended by 43 percent of Finnish high school students, who prepare to work in restaurants and hospitals or at construction sites.

Finnish students consistently score higher on reading, math, and science tests than American students. Can the United States learn from a country of only 5.4 million people? Neighboring Norway, a country of similar size, embraces education policies similar to those in the United States. It employs standardized exams and many teachers without master's degrees. And like America, Norway's PISAS scores have been stalled in the middle ranges for the better part of a decade.[9] (The Program for International Student Assessment, PISA, is an international assessment that measures fifteen-year-old students' reading, mathematics, and science literacy every three years and also includes measures of general or cross-curricular competencies, such as collaborative problem solving.)

During this present decade, our government officials have attempted to introduce marketplace competition into public schools. In recent years, a group of Wall Street financiers and philanthropists, including Bill Gates, have put money behind private-sector ideas, such as vouchers, data-driven curriculum, and charter schools, which have doubled in number in the past decade. President Obama, too, has apparently bet on competition. His Race to the Top initiative invited states to compete for federal dollars using tests and other methods to evaluate teachers, a philosophy that would be anathema in Finland.[10] And Head Start programs, while necessary and worthwhile, have not demonstrated the expected long-term impact. The gulf between education in the United States, with its unique problems, and in other countries is not as much a matter of spending or of better government management as it is a matter of cultural philosophy and priorities.

What is patently clear is that American schools and society are failing its disadvantaged students more than we may realize. We have to acknowledge one unassailable fact. American students painfully lag their peers in other rich nations and even measure up poorly compared with students in some less advanced countries. Americans scored more than halfway down from the top in the last round of the PISA standardized tests in math when compared to sixty other countries, one-third of the way down in reading, and almost halfway down in science. While our educational dilemma is multivariate and complex, this lackluster performance does reinforce the belief that this inequality in American public education is the responsibility of everyone involved, from politicians and school boards to principals and teachers. This begs the question, What is wrong with the system in the United States where so many others succeed?[11]

It is within this context of rising inequality that US poverty, its correlates and consequences, is brought into sharper focus. In 2017, 12.3 percent of the US population, or 39.7 million people, lived below official poverty thresholds. Close to one in five children were poor in 2017, with children of color experiencing higher rates of poverty than white children. In 2017, 91 percent of students attended public schools. During this same year, families headed by single mothers had some of the highest poverty rates. In 2017, 18.5 million people in the US experienced deep poverty. This translates to annual income of approximately $9,757 for a family of three, refuting the stereotype that US poverty is not characterized by significant material hardship. Social science has long been concerned with the short- and long-term effects of childhood poverty on academic performance, educational attainment, socioemotional development, health, and emotional well-being. Researchers agree that school quality, educational attainment, and delinquency were key contributors to economic well-being. A quality education is seen as a major contributor providing disadvantaged children with an increased probability of economic well-being. However, those in disadvantaged neighborhoods are likely to experience not only inferior schools but social isolation with reduced service access, limited economic opportunity, and disparities in the criminal justice system. Discrimination, both overt and covert, are additional barriers to children's opportunities and life satisfaction.[12]

Sociologists have coined the term *achievement gap* to describe the difference in educational achievement between students from different groups. To illustrate, in the entire United States only 3 percent of eighth graders scored at the advanced reading level on the NAEP exams (congressionally mandated National Assessment of Educational Progress exams). The above data substantiate without question the persistent achievement gap between white and minority students. Many inner-city schools languish due to insufficient resources and funding. This sets up a cycle whereby the more affluent move to the suburbs, in part for the schools, thereby reducing tax revenues for the city. Wealthier families that elect to remain in the city may send their children to private schools rather than investing time and money in supporting local schools.[13]

Our government, along with private individuals recognizing the multiple needs of public education, has attempted to address the insufficiencies. Unfortunately, most attempts have proved inadequate.

Many students, parents, and teachers see No Child Left Behind (NCLB) as a detriment to public education. While the Obama administration worked to reform NCLB policies, the focus in education on both the national and state levels continued to be on the testing process. Student test scores were being used by a number of states as a way to evaluate teacher performance. This put more pressure on faculty in schools to "teach to the tests." A major criticism has been, there is really no point to testing as the data are not used to remediate those whose performance is poor.

NCLB was eventually repealed, and Race to the Top fared no better. It forced state governors to put pressure on teachers to test their students so that they might obtain a few years of extra educational funding. Many teachers felt they had to have "dishonest performance lessons" to save their jobs. The underlying complaint is that the government will have to give up control of public education and stop dangling money over their heads in an attempt to push the one-size-fits-all while the testing agenda is really only an attempt to make politicians look good.[14]

Leaders in the Bill and Melinda Gates Foundation have stated, "The United States must recognize that its long-term growth depends on dramatically increasing the quality of its K–12 public education system." By 2018, if today's college graduation rates hold as steady as they have for decades, the US will be short at least 3 million college-educated workers for the projected 101 million jobs that will require a degree.[10]

Title 1, or the Elementary and Secondary Education Act (ESEA), represents the largest investment to schools. It provides funding to states and districts to improve education for disadvantaged students. The Brookings Institute reports its funding per student is quite low and, until recently, averaging about $500 to $600 a year. And there is little evidence that the overall program is effective. Its funding of teacher professional development has been shown to be unproductive, and teachers themselves do not find the professional-development aspect worthwhile. Other services on which principals spent Title 1 funds include after-school and summer programs, technology purchases, and supplemental services, which also have been shown not to be productive.

Title 1 has a sixty-year history. Funds flow to districts based on their counts of students in poverty, which is determined by the Census Bureau. Districts determine which schools get funds by rank-ordering schools based on poverty levels. Once funds arrive at a school, they are used for students at risk of failing to meet state learning standards. An individual student's poverty level plays no role in determining whether the student is eligible for Title 1 services.

We have seen an established correlation between poverty and student achievement. Title 1 no doubt serves students who are poor and underperforming. But the school lunch program does not measure the calorie intake of low-income students and gives their lunches away if low-income students appear to be getting enough calories. In 2015, the National Assessment of Education Progress reported that the average fourth grader eligible for free lunch scored 209 in reading and the average fourth grader who was ineligible for free lunch scored 237. This is how Title 1 treats a low-income student who is making satisfactory academic progress.

Actually, Title 1 until recently had a budget of $14 billion a year, and this really is insufficient. The threshold for operating a Title 1 schoolwide program is that 40 percent of a school's students are eligible for a free or reduced-price lunch. However, current data show that 51 percent of students are eligible.

Eighty-four percent of the money a school receives is spent on instruction and professional development. Follow-up studies found no evidence of effective professional development programs. Two large and rigorous studies of professional development conducted by the Institute of Education Sciences—one focusing on reading and the other math—likewise found no evidence that intensive professional development improved student achievement and evidence that teachers mostly disliked professional development as the activities failed to address their needs.

It is patently clear that if we want to close achievement gaps, Title 1 policy needs to provide sufficient funding, clear definitions and metrics for desired outcomes, and better guidance about effective programming. There has to be continued investments in research to identify effective and ineffective programs. The Senate appears to be moving in this direction.[15]

It must be pointed out that additional federal education programs funding has been overlooked by districts in search of sources for prevention. Impressive strides have been made in the development of evidence-based programs and practices that enhance the behavioral, social, and emotional health of the most vulnerable youth. Several of these programs, particularly social and emotional learning (SEL) programs, and practices have demonstrated a capacity to improve both educational performance and emotional/behavioral functioning. The majority of these programs are part of the Elementary and Secondary Education Act of 1965 (ESEA), which was most recently amended in 2002 by the No Child Left Behind Act. There are approximately twelve ESEA programs with explicit authority for prevention-related activities and three ESEA programs with implicit authority for prevention-related activities.

Conspicuously absent from these well-intentioned programs is the critical area of parent involvement. Teachers report that some parents won't be seen for the entire school year, no matter what issues arise. Others never seem to go away. There are ways parents can become involved and support their child's education, but this does not lend itself to an easy solution. I will address this issue in subsequent chapters along with student attitudes and behaviors, including apathy, tardiness, disrespect, and absenteeism, behaviors seen more frequently at the secondary school level rather than the primary grades.

Additional factors contributing to student failure include the lack of early stimulation during the first five years of a child's life. As a result, many disadvantaged elementary pupils are simply not prepared to meet the educational and social demands of the school environment. These developmental delays often manifest as difficulty in learning as well as adjustment problems. Chapter 6 will address this issue.

Many lower-income neighborhoods where the tax base has declined experience school closings. This often results in other schools being overcrowded. School spending is stagnant and there is a lack of teaching innovation. Early experiences with or an overreliance on technology seems to have a downside in that it forces teachers to change teaching styles to a more quick and entertaining manner, similar to the impact of video game technology.

Many students are lost to the school-to-prison pipeline. Tragically, over half of black young men who attend urban high schools do not earn a diploma. Of these dropouts, nearly 60 percent will go to prison at some point. This statistic is eerily the same for young Latino men.[16]

Without a commitment to a genuine overhaul of public education, we will continue to live with the truism "The more things change, the more they stay the same."

However, readers, do not be overwhelmed by these statistics. This data offers targets for your efforts. As you will see, you have the potential to change lives in a most positive direction. And in your classroom, one student at a time, is where the seeds of change are sown.

3

USING LIFE EXPERIENCES TO MAGNIFY YOUR CREATIVE TALENTS

To FULLY APPRECIATE THE PERNICIOUS EFFECTS stemming from the abysmal failure of public education, it helps to experience it on a personal level. Everyone reading this chapter has a plethora of life experiences with associated knowledge and emotions that permit them to enlist strong identifications with their students' stage of life. When communicated with sincerity, trust develops along with a desire first to please the teacher by mastering what is being taught. If handled correctly, students ultimately shift the goal to taking pride in their own accomplishments. *The key here is the communication of caring.* Without this, classroom success will necessary be limited. It helps to remember that in many ways it is easier to be an adult than a student. If you, the teacher, want a day off because you are tired or have something else to do, you make a phone call and have the day to yourself. If a student does not want to complete an assignment because of simply being tired of the repeated school demands, he or she cannot easily say, "I was honestly too tired and just could not do it."

A number of years ago I was substitute teaching a two-hour physics class when I noticed one of the students fast asleep for the entire class. I honestly felt anger, which I kept to myself for the entire two periods. After the class was over, the student still asleep, I woke him and mentioned his sleeping. He apologized, saying, "After school I work until four a.m. and then go home until I leave for school at seven." I felt ashamed because I realized my anger was based upon "Who does this kid think he is, ignoring me, God?" I looked at him and said, "No problem, you needed the sleep more than the class."

I have for more than forty years had the opportunity to work with and teach inner-city students in public schools, in hospitals, and in conducting educational research. Many of these experiences hold significant relevance for this and the following chapters. These events had a most profound impact on my past behavior as well as continuing to influence my present intellectual and emotional life. Our experiences have much in common. While it is true our paths in life may have been different, it is also true that all our experiences involve others. And if we are able to extrapolate from these encounters, we find there is, as I said in chapter 1, one veritable problem, and that is the problem of human relations. The following vignettes will serve to further introduce me, but more importantly, reveal those experiences that shaped my thinking and beliefs. To become better at what we do, we must leave ourselves open to experiencing. Many of these experiences were quite emotional, and I have heard some say, "Don't become emotionally involved with your students." I really take issue with this absurd notion as the most profound lessons of our lives have an emotional component. How can you truly care about those you teach of there is no emotional involvement? If you want to be a successful teacher, you better love teaching.

In 1969, I finished my master's degree at Temple University, a major university in North Philadelphia. Wikipedia describes North Philadelphia today as "arguably the most dangerous neighborhood in the city. Murders and crime are often associated with gang violence and drugs. It is not wise to venture off main streets. The area around Temple University is very dangerous." I am not sure this would have been an accurate description during the years I worked in this section of the city; at least, I did not initially perceive it in those terms.

Almost immediately after graduation, I was offered a half-time position at Temple University Hospital in the Department of Rehabilitation Medicine. My responsibilities included the evaluation of stroke patients, counseling para- and quadriplegics, and assessing and treating cognitive deficits associated with brain injuries and various other illnesses, including substance abuse disorders. The entire staff, professional and nonprofessional, were wonderful to work with. They loved teaching and learning and constantly communicated their commitment and talents to the patients we were privileged to treat.

At that same time, I also obtained a half-time position at Goodwill Industries, a national and international company whose mission was to help people overcome personal and environmental challenges to build skills and find employment, the goal being to strengthen communities through selling donations of used clothes, household goods, bric-a-brac, and so on.

On one occasion Goodwill decided to start a school to train secretaries in the heart of North Philadelphia. After renting a vacant store, they filled it with the newest in electric typewriters (precomputer days), copiers, chairs, desks, and all that was felt to be needed to train secretaries. The day after the delivery of these items, they were all stolen. The only thing that remained was a note indicating that if Goodwill would pay those responsible $400, all items would be returned. Because my position at Goodwill involved counseling former felons, drug abusers, and others with serious personal and social problems, I was asked to deliver the cash to the now empty store. My response was, this made no sense as the stolen equipment was worth thousands of dollars, and I suggested the police should be involved. Goodwill rejected this idea as they did not want to weaken their position in the neighborhood. I understood and asked one of the men in my group therapy, who himself was a convicted felon, to accompany me while I returned the money. This man had been in prison and had an inoperable bullet still lodged in his brain. Before we arrived at the store, my companion asked that we stop at his home, where he placed a pistol in his pocket. I asked him why he needed it as he was from the same neighborhood. His reply was sobering. "When I was in the gangs, I would have to have a reason to shoot, but this is not true today, and you can be shot for no apparent reason at all."

We dropped off the $400, and the only item returned was a metal typewriter table that had no value and probably could not have been sold. Needless to say, the secretary school never opened. Given limited educational and vocational opportunity, many feel their survival depends on using any means, even if the means fall outside the law or the larger societal norms. I came to understand that many, *but not everyone*, living in North Philadelphia believed they had to develop their own set of acceptable behaviors in order to survive. It started me thinking: Is it fair to take a weapon away from a student who on his way to school has to cross different turfs (neighborhoods) as the weapon might be his only chance of survival? I am against students carrying weapons, but then I did not live in North Philadelphia, where the rules of life and survival are based on a different reality.

Eventually, Temple Hospital turned my position into a full-time one and I resigned from Goodwill. I have already described my responsibilities, but I also worked closely with the transportation orderlies, who were responsible for bringing patients, in wheelchairs or gurneys, from different departments to the physical and occupational therapy areas. I had a close relationship with these young men who were hired from the North Philadelphia area. One afternoon, one of the orderlies came to my office and told me he'd had thoughts about killing people. As I listened, I realized he was quite paranoid and dangerous. I immediately went to my administrator and informed him of the necessity for this orderly to have a medical leave so that I might hospitalize him. The suggestion was rejected because "the orderly [was] black and it would appear that we were picking on him because of his color." I replied, "His color is not the issue, his mental health is, and he is dangerous." Again, the administrator, a lawyer by training, refused to grant a medical leave.

Using Life Experiences to Magnify Your Creative Talents

The only option open to me was to escort this orderly to outpatient psychiatry for treatment.

The next day as I was in a medical staff meeting with residents, we heard shots. This orderly had shot a fellow worker, who then tried to crawl to the emergency room but died. The shooter left the hospital and on his way home shot three more individuals without any fatal injuries. He was arrested at his home, where he had gone to reload his pistol. In his pocket, the police found a list of potential victims. The system failed because of unequal treatment based on the race of a person. Reverse discrimination is no better than discrimination and, in this case, proved to be more dangerous.

At Temple Hospital, I worked closely with paralyzed gang victims. I frequently had to go into a recovery room and tell the patient, most often a gang member, that his spine was severed and that it was unlikely he would ever walk again. This was the essential message, but I tried to present it in a softer way than the above sentence suggests. Usually, when I went into the recovery room, a police officer would be stationed in front of the door. This was not uncommon, for if the rival gang realized their victim was still alive, they often came into the hospital to "finish the job." Once in the patient's room, it was common to have four of the patient's gang guarding each corner of their member's bed. I would ask the four to stand on one side, and I would speak to the patient from the other side of his bed, preparing him (only males during my tenure at Temple) for rehabilitation. Once on the rehabilitation floor, I would see that person in both individual and group therapy. Eventually, I also developed a group therapy with only paralyzed gang victims. All were in wheelchairs, and at times, the interactions became intense. There might be an individual in the group who had shot another in the same session. I never deliberately arranged this, but some of the group members came from other hospitals for these therapy sessions, and their injuries but not their histories were known to me.

At that time, it was not unusual for a paralyzed patient to spend up to one year in the hospital. During this time, you became close to these individuals as they shared their lives with you. One such young man, John, and I became quite close as he was intelligent and had an engaging personality. He had been paralyzed in a stabbing but was motivated for rehabilitation and generally did not exhibit significant signs of depression. He eventually learned to walk with long leg braces, a most difficult task as it requires significant strength and tremendous effort. While there was mutual respect, I felt that my therapeutic efforts toward redirecting his talents and innate attributes met with failure. Upon discharge, I remember saying to him, "John, you won. I did not help you, but I feel we both lost." He assured me this was not the case, and he expressed appreciation for my efforts. I felt he was simply being polite.

Almost one year went by and I was preparing to leave Temple Hospital to study for my PhD as I had received an offer from the University of Pennsylvania to become a teaching fellow. Shortly before I left, I received a call from John's mother indicating he was back in the hospital and had asked to see me. He had been given last rites and his funeral had been planned, but she asked if I would see him if I had the time. His heart had stopped secondary to being caught in the cycle of drug abuse.

I immediately found his room, sat on his bed, and listened to him as he thanked me for what I had tried to do for him when he was a patient. I thanked him, but added that I could think of no reason for him to die and asked him to try to live. The next day I returned to find that John had improved to the surprise of his physicians, and this improvement continued. Eventually, I asked if he would consider making a videotape of what it was like to grow up in North Philadelphia and be a gang member and the role that school had played in his life. He agreed but was hesitant in one respect. Many gang members worked in the hospital, and he was afraid if they saw him making a tape, they would kill him. Eventually, he was carried by me and a hospital engineer down a back stair tower into the basement of the hospital, where we made the tape. He was twenty years old at the time.

Using Life Experiences to Magnify Your Creative Talents

John and his younger brother were raised in North Philadelphia in a single-parent family. His mother was hard working and tried to provide the two boys with the basic necessities of life in a warm and nurturing family without a father. Academic achievement was not a problem in the elementary years. He acknowledged carrying guns to school for self-protection because his schools were often out of his immediate neighborhood. By the age of twelve, John started to become involved with gangs, describing his involvement as a kind of "basic training." At age fifteen, he became a warlord—a gang leader—because he exhibited an aggressiveness that brought him prestige. As a warlord, he had to be consulted before "actions were taken." He admitted having shot to kill because he was shot at and having participated in firing shotguns into groups at parties.

Shortly after age fifteen, he was arrested and jailed at Glen Mills for fifteen months. The charges were for weapon offenses in addition to assault and battery. He described an absence in prison of any vocational training or rehabilitation in preparation for any type of future occupational success. John described the staff as being untrained themselves. A hierarchy rapidly developed in prison, with John describing himself as a "shot," a boss who has "dopes" do their bidding. A third group, the "exiles," those who want no part of gang activities, are left alone.

While John was in Glen Mills, his younger brother, while mailing a letter, was shot in his side. The individual who shot him was placed in the same cottage with John, who wanted to avenge his brother. John gave up on this idea as he came to realize the individual who did the shooting was a coward.

Upon discharge, John entered the Job Corps in Kentucky, which he actually enjoyed very much. He described the experiences and the traveling as meaningful with an absence of any gang activities or fighting. He took a leave of absence on December 16, 1970, to spend Christmas with his family. He was happy visiting relatives until December 29, when his mother asked him to get her a money order to pay some bills. John left home, went to the store, and, not thinking, crossed the wrong turf. He described being surrounded by a bunch of thugs from a former rival gang. He explained that he was on leave from the Job Corps and had not been in the neighborhood for two years. He was almost immediately hit over the head with a whiskey bottle, which dazed him, and then, as he tried to cover his face with his arms, he was stabbed in the stomach five times. Without realizing he was hurt until his arms fell at his side, awake, he dropped between two cars. The gang ran, leaving John on his face and unable to move. One individual returned, and John turned his head and looked at the person as he was stabbed four times in his back. This is what initially brought John to Temple Hospital, where I was to meet him.

During this taping, I asked John about the role of school in his life. He stated that schoolteachers and administrators exhibited an "I don't give a shit" attitude. There was no real interest in students, and if he went to the counselor for a part-time job, it was no use. "After seventh grade the subjects in school were worthless," he said. "We had to learn from the streets as many of us were brought up without fathers and young males don't go to moms but take their problems to the streets, where everyone is looking for a father image as it is not at home or in school." This need to belong and be cared about, while an illusion, was satisfied through relationships with other gang members, but eventually, "they don't really care." John added that his younger brother had returned to finish high school but stopped shortly before graduation because "no one was interested in him as a person."

John, at age twenty, described himself as a physical mess who was unable to satisfy a woman. He was confused, depressed, and overwhelmed about facing society in a wheelchair. He expressed concerns about the future generation of children, who at ages seven and eight were carrying knives and guns, and the nine-to-twelve-year-olds were looking up to their older gang members to be like them—bums and drugs addicts. I was impressed that he worried about the future generation that might have the terrible experiences he'd had. For me, a common thread in the above experiences was a lack of options that might have been available to these young men if they had had meaningful educational opportunities.

It is disheartening to report that, despite my best efforts, I was unable to determine what happened to John in the intervening years since the tape was made. His concern that things were going to worsen testified to his prescience as evidenced in the following paragraphs.

The following material adds to our awareness of the reality of the lives of those who have been and are disadvantaged or neglected. I include this material so the reader may derive a verbal portrait that requires their adding innovative, correcting brushstrokes.

In 2019 in Philadelphia reported 356 deaths by shootings. Among these deaths were over one hundred children. Statistics for shootings without death are difficult to obtain. However, since President Kennedy was shot and killed in late 1963, more Americans have been killed by gunfire in this country than died in all United States–involved wars.[17]

The suicide rate is increasing and is the tenth leading cause of death in this country. Each year 44,965 Americans will die by suicide, and rates of completed suicide jump sharply during adolescence.[18]

In 1971 Helen Oaks wrote in her excellent newsletter that each year in Philadelphia three thousand high school students became pregnant. In a ten-year period, there would be thirty thousand babies born to school-age girls. Ten thousand of these would be born to girls sixteen or under, and 1,500 born to girls still in junior high. With education and contraception, this trend has fortunately changed, and in 2013 the teenage pregnancy rate reached its lowest level since 1990.

Still, 89 percent of teen births are to unmarried mothers, which begs the question, What is the future of a child whose teen mother has a limited and inadequate education? Teen mothers are more likely to drop out of high school, and many teen parents do not have the intellectual or emotional maturity that is needed to provide for another life. According to the National Campaign to Prevent Teen Pregnancy, nearly one in four teens are likely to drop out of high school.[19]

On a tragic note, the Centers for Disease Control and Prevention reported that more than 70,200 Americans died in 2017 from drug overdoses. It is estimated that, on average, there are 7,800 new users per day with more than half being under eighteen. This translates to 192 deaths every day, with the numbers rising.[20] Clearly drug abuse, and its consequences, is of epidemic proportion. How much of this is due to social influences, poverty, or educational and vocational inequality is difficult to determine, but it is obviously significant according to data from a variety of researchers.

It is equally difficult to determine the extent that drugs and alcohol play in the commission of crime. However, when you add up the crimes committed because of the influence of alcohol or drugs, drug-related criminal offenses, and crimes in which illegal possession of a drug itself is the crime, the role of alcohol and drugs in crime is extensive.[21] Spending on illicit drugs in the United States in 2019 neared $150 billion,[22] though alcohol use is decreasing. While this may be due to several factors, such as the easier availability of cheaper drugs, the fact remains that 1.5 million drivers per year are arrested for driving under the influence in the United States. Someone dies every forty-eight minutes in alcohol-related crashes. In poorer areas, when drugs are not readily available for a variety of reasons, alcohol often becomes the drug of choice. John would probably not be shocked by the above statistics, but I believe he would be upset for his brothers and sisters and agree that unmerited misery should offend us all!

One of the most poignant experiences of my career occurred when I was working on my PhD dissertation. I had previously, while working at Temple Hospital, developed an attention-training technique designed to help brain-damaged adults attain sustained attention. This in turn would permit them to bypass injured parts of their brain and achieve greater voluntary control over motor behaviors. I was reasonably successful, and now, working with children, thought, with modifications, the technique could be employed to help the learning-impaired, impulsive pupil.

I was given permission by the Philadelphia Board of Education to conduct my research. I requested the poorest academically performing elementary school in the city. The school was located in West Philadelphia in a most impoverished urban area. Many of the pupils came to school with torn clothes and shoes. Federal money was allocated for clothing as well as lunches. I witnessed those adults responsible for providing clothing to be irresponsible. At the end of the school day, these elementary school youngsters were not permitted to leave the building until all the teachers had driven away in an attempt to reduce aggression toward the teachers and their cars.

My research involved teaching first-, second-, and third-grade students who were described as being in the bottom of their respective classrooms and having questionable ability to achieve. I would take ten students at a time into a separate room for attention training.[23] (The attention training program is included in the appendix.)

One seven-year-old male student was quite friendly and really a most pleasant child. He would often hang around me even after the training was over. Kevin was often late for the start of school as he was responsible for bringing his younger sister to kindergarten. After the ten-minute training session, Kevin and I would often talk. One morning, he told me his uncle had shot someone because that individual had disrespected a relative of his. I'm sure my expression communicated some normal shock to this, but this little child of seven looked at me and said, "He only shot him in the leg." Kevin could not understand my overreaction, and I had to think about his. After all, "it was only his leg!"

As we continued to speak, I asked him what he wanted to be when he grew up. Like many other children, Kevin said, "A fireman." He immediately added, "But I won't make it." I asked him why not, and he replied, "Someone will shoot me." He said it in a way that gave me chills, as though this seven-year-old believed it was inevitable. It is then one begins to realize the insidious effect of poverty, of discrimination, of what it really means to be underprivileged and a student of color in America. Our public education system is a fiction for these students.

John and Kevin are correct and speak for thousands of student-victims throughout our country. Given the disparities in education and the awareness that the system is failing its students, who then is responsible in our society for stopping the perpetual inequalities across lines of race, ethnicity, and class?[1]

Yet we continue to speak of lofty goals: "As our civilization grows in complexity, as the ramifications of our social and industrial life become more extended, as production becomes more specialized and the capacity to change vocations more limited, our political life becomes wider and the duties and obligations of citizenship more important. As our place in the world affairs becomes larger, as the privileges conferred and the responsibility for proper living resting on each individual in society increase, the nature and extent of the education offered as preparation for life must correspondingly increase."[24]

Equal opportunity in education does not imply there will be no differences in individuals' abilities. Differences between humans can simply be accepted as differences and not as deficits. If there are alternative ways of being successful within the society, then differences can be valued. We must not brand people or professions as elite or ordinary. To complement equality of opportunity we need equality of status. Manual labor is not intrinsically inferior to intellectual labor, as I pointed out in chapter 1. Only in a society of equal opportunity for all, regardless of race or class, will every individual have a chance to use his or her full potential. Yet, despite acknowledgment of this truism and the promises of equal educational opportunities, the reality is the death of an illusion.

One final word in this chapter for those who have the courage to climb into the trenches and help correct America's shame: Your ideas, your efforts, your creativity, and even your accomplishments may not always be appreciated by others, whether they be teachers, administrators, or even parents. If you have been honest with yourself and have left yourself open to experiencing and have been open to accepting correctives to your thinking, then above all trust yourself and your creative efforts. I encourage administrators and principals to encourage and support the creative aspects of their faculty. Once these innovations have been found to be of value, then share these changes with others. Change, as you will see, comes through evolution, not revolution. Chapter 2 presented many hundreds of years of educational philosophies, and still no equality in public education for everyone.

4

CREATING CLASSROOM TRUST AND CONFIDENCE: A BLUEPRINT FOR ACHIEVEMENT

IN 1967, after I completed my undergraduate education at Temple University, I was offered an assistantship for my master's degree in the graduate School of Education at the same university.

After two months in this program, I realized that, despite the promise to meet my needs, this program was not for me. I was twenty-nine years old and had been self-supporting since graduating high school. Without this assistantship I was broke. In order to find work, I moved my psychology classes to evening hours. During my undergraduate years I had substitute taught in both elementary and high schools in Philadelphia and truly enjoyed these experiences. Luckily, there was an opening for a long-term substitute position in the counseling department at a large vocational high school near Temple University. I applied for the position and was accepted, in March 1967, at the Muriel Dobbins Vocational School.

Dobbins is both an academic and a vocational high school located in North Philadelphia. This seven-story school offered, at that time, vocational programs in welding, foundry work, commercial and advertising arts, business education, and cosmetology in conjunction with an academic curriculum.

Their counseling department was relatively large with three other counselors; I was the fourth. The head of this department was a talented gentleman who consistently expressed a genuine interest in the students and the school. When I reviewed my counseling list, I also looked at their grades, and if I saw that a student was failing but not a discipline problem, I sought out that student and asked what I might do to help. Doing this, I believed, helped prevent potential problems. After school I might, for example, tutor in geometry or offer support for personal issues. During regular school hours, I focused on the many problems that adolescents have, including disruption and depression and its expressions. After about one and a half months, the counselor whom I substituted for returned and I had to leave this position. However, the head counselor came to me and said the school did not want to lose me and asked if I would accept another long-term substitute position in a specific subject area. I thanked him, and from the subject areas offered, I selected eleventh- and twelfth-grade English.

The morning before I was to meet with my students, I met with the teacher who had been covering those classes I was assigned to teach. He gave me his roll book, adding, "You inherited terrible failures." I felt this unnecessary description was quite inappropriate and unprofessional. It told me more about him as a teacher. Eventually, this impression proved to be accurate.

I then met with the head of the English department, who gave me keys to my room and the curriculum goals, and she repeatedly stressed that I was to teach several of Shakespeare's plays to both grade levels. The reader may have guessed it was this moment that prompted my thinking, it is easier to cram Shakespeare than to produce a Shakespeare.

There were approximately sixteen to thirty-six students in each of three eleventh- and one twelfth-grade classes. Black and Hispanic students comprised about 95 percent, equally divided between males and females, with the remaining students being white—a total of eighty-seven students.

With my roll book, I entered my first class, on my first day, and introduced myself to the students, who sat quietly at their desks no doubt wondering who I was and what it was going to mean for them. I sensed much more, however. Their stares and silence communicated a sense of futility and an awareness of a lack of power to do anything, but having to attend a meaningless class with an unknown teacher.

After introducing myself, I checked roll in an attempt to put a face with a name, but at the same time noticing that almost everyone was either failing or barely passing. I asked them to tell me what they were doing in class. Writing was not emphasized, and a ubiquitous fear of the deadly red pencil often painted their efforts. There was no class discussion, an absence of individual opinions, and little encouragement to challenge the curriculum that they had to adhere to. This described what I experienced in all four of my classes. Their experiences in the English department were anything but gratifying. I went home that evening to think about what I might do to ignite self-confidence, self-respect, and the courage to think independently and express their thoughts. I enjoy Shakespeare, but I have the self-confidence that enables me to express my opinions without fear of being wrong. So, there would be no Shakespeare for the remainder of this term, which was about three-plus months. It would be replaced with the goals influenced by my beliefs and outlined at the end of chapter 1.

The next day, in all four classes and in front of the students, I destroyed the pages in the roll books that recorded the failing grades. This met with mixed emotions of relief and mistrust as I added that all students were not only passing English but with high grades. Continuing, I said there would be a few but enforceable rules that I was adamant about: No one was permitted to make fun of another student's efforts. If you were absent from school, I had to document this; but if you elected to cut my class, you would not be reported to the disciplinarian—you were on your own. If you disrupted class to the extent that it interfered with other students, you were to leave class, and again, you were on your own. In addition, I instructed them not to bring English books to class; I would make up the entire curriculum for the remainder of the term. The reward was coming to class. I realized I was blatantly disregarding school policies, but I honestly believed there was a greater need and obligation that had to be met.

I closed each class that second day with a "public interview." These were the rules: I would ask ten questions that one was free to answer or not; to pass simply say, "I pass." The other students were not permitted to comment, and the student interviewed was free to ask me the same ten questions. Questions in subsequent interviews would change as trust developed and I sensed there were shifts in students' needs. The following is a typical interview[25]:

1. Please introduce yourself.

2. Did you ever get teased? Ever tease others?

3. What does *love* mean to you?

4. Do you believe in premarital sex?

5. Would you bring up your children differently from the way you were raised?

6. Did you ever steal anything? Recently? How come?

7. How do you feel about the mixing of different racial or ethnic groups?

8. How do you personally feel about this issue?

9. Do you do things to make your family or friends feel good without them asking? If so, what and when?

10. Are there things about yourself you would like to change? Would you care to talk about these things?

11. What do you see yourself doing five years from now? Ten years?

12. Can you think of something you would be willing to say to the group that you think might be good for us to hear? (I would always end these interviews with this.)

Initially, when I asked for volunteers, one or two hands went up. In time, almost everyone in all four classes would jump at the chance to be interviewed.

The following is a partial list of the authors, poets, and musicians we read, listened to, and discussed:

- George Orwell
- Bob Dylan
- John F. Kennedy
- Countee Cullen
- Langston Hughes
- Lenny Bruce
- Henry Miller
- Oscar Brown Jr.
- Angela Langsbury
- James Baldwin
- Anne Frank
- Adolph Hitler
- J. Edgar Hoover
- Carl T. Rowan
- Bruno Bettleheim

I would say emphatically to all students, "Each of you is worth more than George Washington, Abe Lincoln, and President John F. Kennedy." Then I would ask, "How can I say this?" Initially, surprise and no response. Then I would add, "Yes, they were great individuals who made their contributions, but they are gone. Each and every one of you is alive and has the opportunity to make your own contribution to life in any number of ways. All you have to do is believe in yourself, trust yourself, think for yourself, and learn to question." This leitmotif was repeatedly woven in multiple ways throughout the time and lessons all classes shared.

While doubt is often the beginning of wisdom, I believe my students came to trust my sincerity. There was one student who would move his desk-chair closer and closer to me as I never sat at my desk but stood in front of it. This student had previously failed English. One day, he came to me and asked if he might tell me something. Facedown and with faltering voice, he told me he was sixteen years old and had a daughter.

He really was unsure of my response, which was, "How lucky you are and how I envy you." I explained that I was, like him, unmarried, but had always envisioned having a daughter. I asked if he had any pictures and if he would share them with his classmates. He did, and in a few days we all became godparents. There is more of this young man's story in the next chapter.

I would read from *Mein Kampf* with the cover concealed and ask, "What do you think about what the author expressed?" I knew there is a human propensity to believe things that are read or told by an authoritative person, such as a writer or teacher or even a parent. And that is what happened. I railed, "Why did you not trust yourself and listen? This lunatic was advocating the extermination of every one of us in this room! Trust yourself." This also was a recurrent theme emphasized in my classes—do not be afraid to form your own opinion, and leave yourself open to new experiences. **In each of you is a treasure chest of talents, emotions, and interests. Please do not be afraid to open this chest. You have an obligation to yourselves to do this.**

I might follow up with this handout (only a short amount is presented here to allow for the readers' take as well):

Our attack on the Hauser-Handlin acculturation thesis, in short, should not lead us into an equivalent blindness on the other side. It should be clear by now that acculturation alone will not solve the Negro problem; without potency it leaves the Negro in a cultural and political vacuum, a no-man's-land, as it were. But power without acculturation can also be a blind alley.

This piece goes on for hundreds of words.

Now, class and readers, what do you think? The answer should be, it is meaningless and absolute gobbldygook. But one must have the self-confidence to trust himself to listen, form, and express an opinion.

There were a few discipline problems, and I would simply ask those students to leave the classroom. However, I would, when possible, seek those individuals during their lunch period, buy them lunch, and talk about life but not their behavior. Invariably, they would say, "You really want me in your class." I would respond, "That is what I have been saying." It took some longer than others to trust.

When I had free periods I would visit my students' vocational classes. For example, I might say to the welders, "I can weld; let us have a contest." Other times found me in the foundry, saying, "You know what I do; I came to learn what you do." I would make sure to attend some of the more vulnerable students' after-school athletic practices.

I told them the story of Joseph Peters, a young man who was kidnapped in Africa and sold into slavery in America. During the Revolutionary War, the British had promised "every Negro that would murder his master and family that he should have his master's plantation." Joseph Peters did not murder anyone, but escaped from slavery and, with three thousand other African Americans, joined and fought for the British for the duration of the war.[26] The question to the class: "Was Joseph Peters a traitor?"

I presented the following poem by Countee Cullen:

"Incident"

Once riding in old Baltimore,
Heart-filled, head-filled with glee,
I saw a Baltimorean
Keep looking straight at me.

Now I was eight and very small,

And he was no whit bigger,
And so I smiled, but he poked out
His tongue, and called me, "Nigger."

I saw the whole of Baltimore
From May until December;
Of all the things that happened there
That's all that I remember

At another time:

"What Is Wrong"

What is wrong with me?
Everywhere I go,
No one seems to look at me.
Sometimes I cry.

I walk through the woods
And sit on a stone.
I look at the stars,
And I sometimes wish.

Probably if my wish ever comes true,
Everyone will look at me.

—Written by a twelve-year-old girl
in Freedom School, Mississippi,
Summer, 1964

Needless to say, the classroom discussion was overwhelmingly impressive and, at times, heated but productive. Students were expressing their thoughts and opinions and defending them with reason and passion in an atmosphere of trust and acceptance. I am not trying to paint an overly Pollyannaish picture, but there were significant changes in all my classes. Attendance was pluperfect, and in fact, students from other grades were now simply attending my classes when they could. Even some high school dropouts from the North Philadelphia area took the time to come and hear what was going on in our classes.

It must be pointed out, I had on several occasions invited the school principal to observe our classes. Unfortunately, he never took me up on this invitation.

They were surprised to learn that I believed the anthropologists' view that the birth of mankind was in Africa. If this was true, why then, as we looked at the pictorial history of blacks in the South, were there thousands of lynchings and burnings? And white parents would bring their children to watch these monstrous events as though they were on a picnic. Students began to introspect as to how they reacted to this history and how their current behavior and attitude toward others was influenced by these past horrors as well as their present lives. We also reviewed biographic briefs of blacks who contributed to the building of our nation in the areas of science, music, government, art, exploration, and social justice to name a few areas that enriched our world.

I felt it was also important for each student to think about what is worthwhile in life. For me, I explained, it is not so much, What do I want to be? but, How do I want to be? at whatever I do. Student interviews periodically continued, and if I forgot and went too long without an interview, some student would remind me.

One doesn't have to look too far for material to challenge or think about values. For example, the leaders of the sporting goods industry found when they put a "famous name" on a piece of equipment, it sells at a substantially higher price than the identical equipment without the name. The question I asked: "Why do you think that putting some famous person's autograph on a particular product should increase sales?" There is no right or wrong answer, just opinions. Life is full of choices. What guides you, the student, when you have to decide? These were additional day-to-day activities in all my classes. I tried to tailor my approach to reach, as much as was possible, all students.

I asked they put themselves in Anne Frank's place. Bruno Bettelheim believed that the Franks denied the reality of the Nazi world around them and should have left their hiding place. The students were divided into small groups to judge whether Bettelheim or Anne Frank made the correct decision. What would they have done? It was impressive to hear the opinions and see how they were unafraid to express their reasons to their classmates.

The Viet Nam conflict and the protests to this war were raging and were clearly on the minds of my students. This was particularly true for the seventeen- and eighteen-year-old pupils who soon might be considered for the draft. We listened to the music of Bob Dylan, Peter, Paul and Mary, and others and discussed the impact of the war on their lives as well as the effect it was having on our nation. These pupils dealt with these events with intelligence and discrimination.

I also explained that not every good deed is rewarded, and at times we do what is correct because it is the right thing to do. What happened to the fifty-six men who signed the Declaration of Independence? I asked. I imagine very few people think about this. Five signers were captured by the British and were tortured and died because they were seen as traitors. Twelve had their homes ransacked and burned, and nine fought and died from wounds or hardships in the Revolutionary War. A large percentage of the fifty-six signers died in poverty. I asked the students, "What might you have done at that time?" adding, "Do you have the confidence in yourselves to take a chance in things you believe to be the right thing?" These were matters to think about and did not require an answer—a kind of homework without the label. Since it was relevant to the lives of each student, it was never seen as homework. I explained how important it is to trust yourself to read and think for yourself and to determine what information is worthwhile, as well as the need to think about the truth of the myriad of taught "facts."

I would cut items from the newspaper and point out, for example, the two articles shown below and ask them to compare them and express their opinions as to what communicated the more worthwhile information.

What War Is

Air Force Maj. Victor Colasuonno wrote a letter from Vietnam to his son and the rest of the fourth grade class at Church of Magdalen Catholic School, Wichita, Kan., in answer to their question of "what war is." "I'll tell you what war is not," the major wrote. "It is not a glamorous, daredevil existence where the 'good guys' always win. It is not a fearless fighter pilot jumping into his airplane to shoot down the enemy. It is not a game which you play and which I played as a child, where you go home to a good supper and a warm bed after it is over. War is fought by real human beings, not Hollywood stars — men like your daddy and perhaps older brothers. War is all the horrible things a human being can do to another human being because he has not learned to love . . . Perhaps your generation can accomplish this — it seems that mine has failed." Maj. Colasuonno, a pilot, was killed in action last

Knee Mending

GINA LOLLOBRIGIDA, who underwent a successful operation on her fractured left kneecap, will be able to leave the hospital in Rome in about ten days, doctors said. A passenger in the car she was driving that crashed was FRANCO ZEFFIRELLI, who produced the film "2001: a Space Odyssey." He also is hospitalized.

Below is a picture also cut from a newspaper showing an unfortunate man, perched on a high building, threatening suicide. The crowd is encouraging him to jump. What do you think of the crowd, and what do you think you might have done if you were in the crowd, and why?

Crowd Urges Man to Suicide

Amos Gexella was perched on a sixth floor balcony in Johannesburg, South Africa. Listening to a man who was trying to talk him to safety, Onlookers below kept calling, "Jump, jump." Gexella finally plunged to his death.

The following is an example of another class exercise:

These are two views of man. Where do you stand, and why?
1. "I beg of you to remember that wherever our life touches yours, we help or hinder. Wherever your life touches ours, you make us stronger or weaker. . . . There is no escape—man drags man down, or man lifts man up."

—Booker T. Washington

2. "The world is beautiful, but has a disease called Man."

—Friedrich Nietzsche

Creating Classroom Trust and Confidence: A Blueprint for Achievement

The atmosphere in our classrooms was now characterized by the trust and actions that reflected blossoming self-confidence, increased responsibility for one's own actions, and, most importantly, a belief in one's own worth as an individual who is willing to express his or her opinions. But could they express themselves in writing?

One day, I told all my students that they would have to pay to attend classes. The pay was in the form of a three-by-five-inch card that I would provide each Friday. On Monday, I would collect the cards, on which I expected them to have written something important to them. It could be one word or sentence, one card or many, and if they had difficulty writing, they could draw something. There were to be no corrections and no assigned grades. I would read a few cards in class unless a student preferred it remain a private communication and indicated this by writing, "Do not read." I added, "Do not worry about spelling, grammar, or syntax; just write about something that is important to you."

The cards poured in. Many were from students who had never written anything as far as I could determine. Often, they would come to me and ask if it was okay to write about personal issues. I replied, "Are you sure you want to write that?" Invariably they said yes.

At the start of Monday's class, I would select a few cards to read only to the class in which the cards were collected; then I would thank the students and genuinely praise their efforts. Their expressions of trust and belief in me were overwhelming. I knew I was responsible for what I had created. The weight of this responsibility obligated me to not only continue earning their trust but somehow make them proud of their own accomplishments by recognizing how far they had come. They took chances. We, as teachers, often forget that is what learning requires. When one is able to open themselves to new learning, one is less afraid to be open to more of life's possibilities.

As the term was drawing to a close, I made this suggestion: why not put a magazine together from all the writings that I had saved to let the other teachers know their thoughts on what they considered worthwhile. At the same time, the magazine would let the faculty know what topics should be discussed at their grade levels and what they were capable of communicating. The response was overwhelmingly positive. The printers volunteered to print the project, the women in the secretarial program would type it, and those in the commercial arts program would draw the cover. The excitement and feelings one gets when one creates a new idea became apparent. These emotions permeated all my classes, and the students were totally self-motivated.

I took my box of three-by-five-inch cards, their tickets of admission, and read every card to all the students, who then voted on those cards they felt belonged in their magazine. I had no part in the selection, and the cards were left uncorrected for spelling and syntax and grammar. I knew there would be some criticism of my not having corrected their writing, but as I previously mentioned, the goal was to get them to trust that they could write about ideas they considered important. Teaching syntax and grammar to me, at this stage, was less of a priority.

My only contributions to the magazine included writing the introduction and suggesting the idea for the cover, the creation of which was in the hands of the commercial art students. I had the habit of arriving at the school early, but now found the young women were in school at 7:00 a.m. typing their magazine. My classes decided they would print approximately 350 copies to be distributed to all teachers and only those students in my classes. The following is my introduction to the magazine "Introspection." (The uncorrected essays that follow are reproduced exactly as they appeared in the magazine, including the typos.)

> The shortcomings in our educational system are most obvious in our secondary schools. Many programs are scaled to the students' several levels of vocational outlook and have little to do with enriching their experiences and helping them lead enjoyable, productive lives. Much of what is taught has been stripped

of its true meaning, and class work is segregated from adolescent social life. Most high schools are in fact institutions of anti-intellectualism.

We, as teachers, with the power of enlisting strong identifications, must reawaken the students' long-lost interest and enthusiasm. The school must harness the adolescent social spirit to the job of teaching and learning. Only in this way can an education become a meaningful preparation for real life and not just a collection of parroted references.

One purpose of this student publication is to inform educators of the wide range of possible topics that can and should be handled in today's classroom. I am of the opinion that students should begin their reading with the literature of their times. [I had presented the previously mentioned list of authors.] Teachers must not slavishly follow a sterile curriculum guide, but ask himself, What is worth teaching, and why do I want the student to learn what I am teaching?

I hope that as one reads this magazine he may derive an appreciation of the passionate social and moral concerns which show how the adolescent views his world.

I added that I would like to thank all the members of my classes for their many contributions to this publication and especially for their patience with me. All the students' names, grade levels, and class periods were listed. The following are many of the students' writings presented exactly as they are in the magazine. (The cover is shown below.)

Reasons for High School Dropouts

1. Broken homes
2. No money for graduation facilities
3. Encouragement from other dropouts

I feel that people should not down the dropout students. I feel they should give them a chance in life, a chance to prove they just didn't drop out because they might have been dumb, or maybe been kicked out. But a chance to prove that they can do good even if they don't or didn't finish school. Sure finishing school could help you to get a good job, but if it is not possible to do so you just can't. I think you should be given a chance to show what you can do.

—by G.B.

The Rules of The Board of Education

Some rules are fine. Sometimes you just have to put your foot down and I know it. But somethings are from the olds. The rules are so old that some older teachers say they remember them when they were children. I think we should really try to do something about it.

—by J.S.

Children love, Adults Hate

A baby does not know what color or race is. A baby has to be taught how to hate or love.

You see little children playing together while they are young but while they grow up the teaching of hate begins. So why if they can play together while they are little, why can't they live together and work together in a grown up world.

—by G.F.

STEVE HARLEM, P.h.D.

The World Problem is Understanding

The world problem I say is understanding. Understanding is a serious problem you might not beware of it but it is a world problem that people will never understand. People in the world are different, not one person looks identical the same. Some people do poor in certain jobs and the boss can't understand why, what makes this man think. This person or persons may slow and can't express himself to the satisfaction of his superior. He may be a man of many problems this all leads to trouble because of not understanding.

—by J.B.

Teenagers of Today

I feel that there is nothing wrong with the styles and character of teenagers of today (not saying this because I'm a teenager myself.) What I'm trying to say is that adults should try to put themselves in the place of teenagers and try to understand and adjust along with criticises the ways of the teenager of today and I'm sure that by doing this it can change the faces of a lot of unhappy parents and teenagers.

—by G.B.

Teachers in Dobbins

The teachers in Dobbins some are strict; the others are too leaneant. Some of them curse, some of them swear, some of them have school spirit and some don't. Some know how to teach and some know how to preach. Some teachers beat the work in you and some work out of you. Some teachers try new teaching methods and some stick with the old methods. Some teachers don't care if you learn or not they say I'll get paid anyway. But most teachers I have are <u>ALLRIGHT.</u>

—by G.F.

Teachers, there are different kinds of teachers. There are teachers who will teach and that's it. But there are teachers who you can talk to and talk about what you would like to learn. And there are teachers like you who you could talk about your school problems outside of school and you would listen and try to help. And talk like your friends would instead of teachers.

—By A.B.

DEATH

Most people say they are afraid to die but I'm not and I feel that if you been doing the right things and have faith in God there is nothing to worry about. So if you haven't been doing the right things, START NOW don't wait until it's too late because there are only two places to go and you know if, you're not going to Heaven you're to go to Hell.

—by G.B.

What is death, it is just the stopping of breathing the opposite of life? This is one experience no living person ever went through thoroughly. Couldn't it be that it is the real beginning of life, a reward from God to those he feels accomplished a certain mission or task on earth. Couldn't death instead of being black and silent be really bright and cheerful. The answer to this I feel is just blowing in the wind.

—By G.B.

RACIAL

Why do the people of the world press the Negro? Every time something happens it seems the negro is involved, on newspaper headlines, newscasts reports, special programs. Today everything is antinegro. Why?????

—By U.J.

Whites in the Way

I know I heard them say there are whites in the way. I knew then I would try to stay. I'll try to avoid a fight with all my might. I know it wouldn't be easy. For there'll be lots of teasings. I know one day someone will say NIGGER STAY OUT OF OUR WAY. And when I turn to go another way I know there will be more whites in the way. But nowhere could he go on stay because there'll always be whites in the way.

— by M.Y.

I am ignorant, I steal, I lie, I cheat. Are these really my characteristics? Can't I be sweet, kind, not steal, not lie, I want to be really liked, to have friends. Are all my people alike? We have education, we have minds, we have a heart a soul, the same as yours. Must you be so cruel old world. Must you make everyone, cry, hush, hate. Can I see your new side? Of all colors.

—Unsigned but I believe it's by M.Y. above

This World I live In

I live in a world full of prejudice and hate which when I entered was doomed for fate. One for a kind, other for another which seems to put, brother against brother. Have not I heard, to hate is a sin, just because of one's color of skin? Is not a black man, as good as a white? Who has the power to put people on sides. No one I say, just a way to show pride. I call this no pride, it should be Shame for this is a loss, not a gain. This world I live in many changes could be done that maybe someday we can be joined as one.

—By M.W.

Instinct of Death

Here I am packed and standing, tomorrow I leave for Veitnam. I kissed my wife, I kissed my kids. For tomorrow I may not live. I have a son, he is three, he may not even remember me. I cry as I sit and bear the thought, these are my last hours, days, maybe months even my thoughts. My heart is heavy, my face full of sweat I'm a negro full of regret. I have a life I haven't lived free. Now I'm going to die, far across the sea.

—By J.T.

The Beginning of Slavery

Once there was a free and happy man, who lived in a far away land. But across the sea were other lands where the men did not like to use their hands. These men were white you see, these men that lived across the sea. They said why should we get down on hands and knees to plow the land and kill the weeds, when there are black men across the sea. We are stronger and can do the work of three. A few months later in the foreign land there was a working, starving, slaving black man.

—by D.W.

Equality

To me equality means to live where you want, to go where you wish, to associate with whom you please, and not be obligated to feel inferior to <u>ANY RACE.</u>

—by R.W.

Integration

I think integration is fine. People get to meet new people and do new things. I can see sending people to different schools nearly to integrate them. But on the other hand I can't see sending people on buses to far away schools just to integrate the schools. I think it's fine as long as they just don't go too far.

—by J.S.

Racial Discrimination

I feel that all this fighting between the white and colored is senseless. The only reason they're fighting is because they don't want colored people in their restaurants and swimming pools, etc. The main reason why white people hate colored is because they want colored people to stay under them. I feel the whole purpose of racial discrimination is the white never want a negro to advance in life to maintain a high standard.

—By M.M.

Why the Negro is Dumb, In Poverty and Degradation
Some reasons (not all)

The negro is denied the right to achieve equality of opportunity by not being able to go to the school of his choice because of his color, and not because of his intelligence. They can't move where there's a all-white family and can't obtain high position because of their color. Without equality of opportunity they can never escape from ignorance, poverty and degradation. There is no true justice for the negro. Negroes are handicapped in many ways. Some are denied the freedom to vote, hold public office, etc.

—by M.Y.

Racial Equality

What is it? Is it defined as a state of being equal to one another. Are all people equal to another? This is one of a thousand questions asked each day. Can a man (negro) buy a home without being persecuted by whites. Is it possible for anyone to go into a public place of buying without ridicule from others. Are all people being treated the same? Are we all protected by the full extent of the law? I wonder? So should you wonder?

—By G.Y.

"ALL MEN ARE CREATED EQUAL"

What makes the Negro different?

—By B.H.

Declaration of Independence and Bill of Rights

Are all men created equal in freedom of speech, freedom religion, and racial tolerance. Is America the cradle of freedom: No, not for the negro, it isn't. American they say live instated in the above factons. Many negroes in the south haven't had the right to share none of these rights. A negro is looked at first a negro and second as an American. The negro problem is now America's greatest failure but if something is done about it, it can be America's greatest success.

—By M.Y.

"Are all Men Created Equally"

If so why is the negro treated as though he is unequal to the white men. The negro is not lok on as a human being, but as a tool of labor. The negro pays the same amount of carfare as the white man, but the negro is expected to move to the back of the bus, while the white man is allowed to sit where he please. Is this equality? No! I'm not ready to surrender a way of life my foefathers founded good and have cherished over the centuries. I will protect myself against any kind of color.

—By M.Y.

Will We Ever Be Free???

Yes you and me, can we ever really say we are free? What are we free of? There is still poverty and ignorance, fighting and destruction, when will we ever be able to walk down any street, without being afraid? I wonder, they say that we have the right to, but do we, I ask myself that many times. But I never get an answer. Why, is such a very big word. So many people ask why, oh god when the hell will I find out. I'm so confused. Will my children have this trouble? Will they too, have to ask Why, or will I be able to answer them? I guess I'll never no, WHY?

—By L.J.

Hate

Well I think that this problem can be stopped only at home. Many children are taught at home how to dislike and feel as if they are superior to people of there races. I know of a few families that actually teach hate to their children.

—by R.C.

Indifference

People have been hanged, burnt and beat too death by angry mobs because of their race and religion. Many people stand by and laugh and some even help in the killings. Things are a little better today. People just stand back and watch people getting robbed, beaten, raped, or killed. Do they do anything about it? Of course not, they don't want to take the law in their own hands.

—By S.S.

WAR

In my opinion we shouldn't be in Viet Nam trying to save them from Communist. To me if South Viet Nam wants to take over North Viet Nam it their country. I can hardly see myself fighting in Viet Nam to free them, when I hardly have freedom over here. I hope the time I go into the service the war with Viet Nam will be over with, if not I don't think I'd risk my life over there trying to free someone else.

—by L.W.

This is what the word war stands for: World wide acknowledged and utterly useless means of getting things accomplished. A, to me, cannibalistic way of settling things. Abundant dead, destruction and plentiful grive for all to see and to hopefully learn from. Relentless heartache and poverty, when it is over man should stop and think and when he does speak the word should be Peace.

—By H.S.

THE SELFISH GOVERNMENT

They shall not kill is what the bible says
But you must say the Government in their world today
People died by the thousands this year
Government sat back and said who cares
For we the government want all the lands
To work out our own selfish plans
To build and construct
To destroy and corrupt
To scare and confuse

To burn and abuse
All those who refuse
To obey our rules
Of destruction
And corruption
For we the Government
Is the judgement
Of who is to life today
And die tomorrow regardless of any amount of sorrow.

—By L.W.

Pre-Marital Sex

It is wonderful if you are mature enough to take the responsibilities that go with it such as, if the girl becomes pregnant or you may get some kind of venereal disease. For me, I dig Pre-Marital sex and I think the world would be a better place if everyone agreed with me.

—By D.T.

ABORTIONS

I am against abortions because I feel that no child that I know of ask to come into the world and if the so called parents of this child do not feel they can't carry out the responsibility of parents they should forget about doing things when it involves a new life into the picture. I think when people do these things they should think about themselves in this predicament, and they would also help lower the number of abortions in our everyday world.

—By G.J.

UNWED MOTHERS

Lots of girls and women have children. It is a big responsibility and its even bigger when you aren't married. If you have a child and isn't married you feel ashame. WHY? You didn't do anything against the law. You become sexually involved with a man or boy and a child came from this. Maybe you don't love him anymore but is that any reason for you to love the child any less. No! You should love and cherish that child as though it were born in wedlock. You should keep and raise him or her to be strong and face life with a reality that everything isn't the way you read about it in books. It's a world where you live your life to the fullest extent. Never be ashamed that you never married the guy just be glad that you have something to remember him by. Maybe one day you'll meet a guy who'll love you and the child and you'll love him and be happy and maybe have too many regrets. It is a human being and ever it is a part of you and someone you loved. Don't give it away and be sorry. Keep the child and be happy for the rest of your life.

—By S.A.H.

SEX
Should it be taught in schools

Yes, sex should be taught in school maybe if it were taught in school there wouldn't be much sex crimes today. If you let people learn what sex is maybe they wouldn't go out on their own and do things which cause them to go to jail. Sex is part of life and all facts of life should be taught to everyone.

—By M.Y.

The sex problem that everyone mostly overlook in the younger adults. It is the fault of the school and parents for not introducing the subject at the proper time. You would be surprised at the many uninformed children who have to find out about sex on their own leading to illegidament children, and diseases. This problem is about the easiest to be solved, with just a little time and concern.

—by J.B.

The abortion laws should be changed. I do not think if you are going to have a baby and you don't want it that you should go out and get an abortion. I do not think this is right. I think only the people involved in rapes should have this abortion, if they want it and people having babies that are going to be deformed and mentally retarded if this is what they want then it is o.k.

—By G.V.H.

1/5/67 My life began today. I don't have any arms or legs yet but they will soon begin to take form. 1/12/67 My legs seem to be coming along very well, soon, in about eight months, I'll be able to walk. 1/20/67 Mommy went to the doctor today, I guess she wanted to know how I was coming along. Well, tomorrow she will tell Daddy, and he will be happy. We will have lots of fun my mommy and I, running and playing in the parks and going on picnics. She doesn't know I am a girl but she'll know soon enough. 1/30/67 I guess my mommy didn't love me enough. Today she stop my life. We would have had so much fun. I didn't even have a chance........

—by G.R.

Every phase of Sex education should be taught in school. I think this should include giving <u>knowledge</u> to both male and female, such as "The Pill", "Abortion", use of "Prophylatics", etc. Students should learn the functions of the parts of the human body in the 5th or 6th grades. Sex education should begin in junior high school. This is about the time when the average pupil becomes a teenage and reaches puberty.

—By S.S.

HOW DO YOU VIEW HOMOSEXUALITY

In my opinion the problem of Homosexuality is a cause of great concern in the U.S. and all over the world. I feel that this problem is a condition of the mind. It is a real evil that men are force by the mind. It is a real evil that men are forced by the people around them to turn to homosexuality as a way of life. Because of having female tendency these men are pushed to the point of no return. As for myself I hate and pity the character of a man who let himself be push into giving up their muscaline qualities.

—By S.S.

I feel that there is nothing wrong with talking about sex. I know some people can't talk about it. I feel they should talk about sex in school because sometimes the parents don't have all the answers to the teenagers questions. If they allowed this in schools maybe we would not have so many teenage mothers they would know in what kind of trouble they would be getting into.

—By T.Z.

I am against Pre-Matrial relations because it causes much pain. To many problems are involved. For some it is love, for some it is just for kicks. Some boys get a thrill out of being the first to "get a girl," and brag about it, But is not always the boys fault.

—By M.S.

MARRIAGE

In my opinion, marriage is very sacred and it is something where two people join themselves in a bond as one. It is not just love of sex because if it is they'll part. But it has to be free love because later in life there will be other problems. And the only thing to life or marriage is not sex. Even though it plays a important role in a marriage.

—by J.T.

MIXED MARRIAGE

I feel it does not matter what race, or religion you are if you want to get married to someone. I feel that if two people are in love with each other it does not matter if their skin is different. People stop and look at the people, start to talking what they don't know. I know quite a few friends which have mixed marriages, and they are getting along fine. My advice is to you to marry who you wish but make sure you love that particular person.

—by T.Z.

Space Program

I think the space program is very necessary, because whoever reaches the moon first can control the world, there might be natural resources we might can use for our benefit. Like they say of television "Space is the last frontier" and whoever owns the moon can use it for a space station for further space exploration. They can study the earth, so I think that the space program is very important. And also they can study other planets and stars more thoroughly from the moon.

—by G.F.

Religion

I feel religions are good in a sense but I think a person of one religion should go into other churches of different kinds and see how they pray etc. People that only know one religion refuse to hear someone speak about their religion.

—by K.H.

Most people say that if you're not the same religion as they are that your religion isn't any good but I feel that everyone is intitled to worship GOD as they wish and in their own way as long as they know that they're getting through to our maker.

—By G.B.

A Child

To me a child is a creation of God, of the love a man and a woman has for each other. A child is like a flower. I can grow to be very beautiful, but it depends on how it is taken care of. A child is beauty at a start just starting to grow.

—by B.H.

Colors

When I was young and very small
I knew not any colors at all
As I became a little older
Colors became a little bolder
When I was small I no not black or white
Now I do not know which is wrong or right.

—by L.H.

Capital Punishment

Is it really necessary to kill another person because they have killed someone else. I can't say Yes or No, but the people selected on these juries can say he must die. What the use in sending a man or woman to the Gas Chamber or the Electric Chair. If these is suppose to be teaching others or warning them that if they commit an unpardonable crime they will die.

Some warning! People are getting killed everyday, some people say an eye for an eye, tooth for a tooth. Why? Revenge perhaps? If not, then what? There was recently a California man tried and convicted of cop-killing. Why must he die? Because he kill someone not just anyone, but a cop, why kill him, send him to jail for the rest of his life. Just knowing he was to spend the rest of his days of earth in a prison cell is enough to drive a man crazy. I believe this would be a better world if Capital Punishment was abolished. The bible says thou shall not kill, so does the law, and they say it is right for them to someone. What makes it right? Who are they to say who will die and who will live. What would they do if they were convicted and sentenced to die. Some states gave decided to do away with it. Why not let other states follow them? Think about this.

—by G.Y.

Hate

I think hate is all in the mind not in the heart. You can't hate a person for nothing. An example of this in Racial problems. I feel that hate in children toward a different race is due to the fault of the parents false teaching.

—By M.S.

People

People, some people are kind and nice and there are some who would stab you in the back if you didn't watch them. The good ones will go out of their way to help you, and do anything for you and be like a brother or sister. Someone you can sit down and talk to and help you with your problems. So I wish everybody would be a good one.

—By A.B.

A friend is someone who shares your interests and feelings. He tries to help you improve yourself without using unkind words. He is there to listen to your problems and help you solve them. He is willing to do things for you without expecting something in return. He enjoys doing things and going places with you. To have a friend you must be a friend.

—By B.H.

Question

Why does the people of the U.S. say that we have equality but to me the Negro has none. Why?

—By U.J.

In the darkness of night
Hark I see a light
As I walk toward the light
I fall in a deep pit with a terrible fright
As I wake up with a shovel
I see I'm shoveling coal for the devil.

—By F.E.

The Future

The future is the desendant of the past, it depends on the past ton exist. That is why it is up to us, the people of today to build, to create, and to secure the world of tomorrow. It is also up to us the people of today to set to set up for the final frontiers of space and under water, and to make a world in which the word war would be extinct.

—By G.B.

Mother

I value my sick mother more than anyone in the world. She has cancer now and my father has to take her every day down to Hamilton Hospital for radium treatment for hopes that it will kill some parts of a second of tumors to be removed. The first one was as big as a fist and it almost killed her and she has to go back to the hospital for the third or fourth operation. She is very weak and is worrying about every little thing. Her biggest worry I hate to say is me because I don't get along because I don't get along too good on the outside. I have to watch myself and everything I say around her, for instance one night I was put in jail, she almost died from pleading to the captain of the fourthteen district to go up to the jail and get my son, so they did and told me next time your mother won't get you off and we're going to send you so far away that you will never see your mother and plus you do the time when your mother got you off and I know that this could kill her.

—By J.B.

Man's Goal

Every man has a goal in life, something to keep him going, no man should be content or fully satisfied with any position in life, meaning if a man is presently a ditch digger he should want to be maybe a leader of a exploration group, exploring underground, what I'm trying to say is everyman should try to better himself grasping every possibility that would improve his present position. A contented man is an unhappy man and a unsatisfied man is a man with an more prosperious future.

—By Anon

Value Cards

Why don't they understand? People are so self-righteous, they never do anything wrong. Of all the things you do they only remember the wrong ones. Why can't remember when they were young, or if they do they always give you the excuse that things were different then. But that's a damn lie. The names and places might change from Germany to Viet am, but its still the same problem. I can't stand to have people say back in my day we had it hard, but I've got it easy. Ha, Ha that's a big laugh, or they give you that old line—these kids now-a-days, I don't know whats going to become of them. I can tell you what will become of them. They will land on the moon, Mars and answer questions that haven't even been thought of yet. They will master the world and even go farther than any one before them I'm proud to be one of them.

—By L.L.

Respect and Our Parents

I feel we should respect our parents the way we want them to respect us. I do not mean in this manner to respect our parents one minute of the day and the rest of the day we can do as we please, but we should respect our parents all the time even if we think they are not being fair. If we look at it from their point of view they're only doing it for our own good. When our parents tell us what to do we should not start asking questions but just start doing the chore. When our parents tell us to be in the house at a certain time we should be in it at that time and not after even if we don't agree with the time they have set for us. We should respect and obey our parents as long as we are under their roof. They're only trying to raise us to be well manners, decent, honorable, young adults. Remember when we're parents we'll want the same respect from our children.

—by J.B.

I would like to put in a good word for high school technical education. It is a very worthwhile thing for those students who know they are not college material. It saves the industry a lot of money on training. It insures the student of a good job after graduation, and a chance to get ahead in the business. Finally, I think that Dobbins is the best place to learn a trade.

—By A.H.

Juvenile Deliquent

A deliquent is usually a boy or girl who is from a broken family or a poverty-stricken family, a rough neighborhood, or maybe he is just misled. He will steal what he wants, he will not use his own backbone to earn money, but waits for someone else do it and the deprives him of the right to love it. He will beat up innocent people, and will do it without very much reason. He will sexually assault a woman without shame or feeling of disjustice. Don't misunderstand me, because all are not very bad, and if taken care of can be stopped in time. I talk about it as if it were a disease, and in some sense it is. The reason I say in some sense it is because of delincuency knows no race, no religion, and rich or poor can be struck by its dreadful finger.

They (and I say they because I am not one) are scorned by most of the general public and not very understood nationally. I deeply feel that a deliquent boy or girl should be taken aside and shown that someone cares, and has an interest in them. I would gladly devote my life to the development of my society. He will wear his big hat, high-top comforts and his terrible language and think that is really something to be proud of. He will carry a gun, maybe even more, but though called, he is not an animal. If the public disowns him they are as savage as they made him. I rest my case.

—By H.S.

DOPE ADDICT

I think people should try and take time out and understand all dope addicts. I feel that taking dope is like a cancer disease once you have it is very hard to get rid of it and most people that don't want to be bothered.

I also feel that people that have this profession in helping dope addicts are contributing much to the society of today and tomorrow.

—by G.B.

I am 15 years old and I am a heavy drinker. I drink almost every night. The only thing I drink is wine. I usually drink about two quarts a night, and I can't stop. I have had blackouts, been rejected by my friends, and I am lonely.

—By A.F.

NARCOTICS

I feel that there is much of this going around. There are many boys and girls taking them. I have seen many girls lose their virginity because they are so called "digging their high." I have been around people sniffing glue, and ruining their lives.

—By M.S.

Killer of disease. If only people would show more concern to the addict and know that he has a disease down in side that has to come out and that disease is: SHAME, GUILT, and PAIN!

—By anon.

In a free society everyone has the right to criticize.

(In this last section the students on their own, as with everything above, wrote to the principal.)

Dear Mr. D.

My letter is based on our system of learning and the teachers system of teaching. Dobbins is receiving new teachers from time to time, these teachers are young with their own ideas. They have just graduated to a stage where they have to accept full responsibility for a class of students. They have just learned the new ideas and basics of teaching.

The teachers at Dobbins who have been here for a while, have set in their mind that their way is right. That their rules are the only and correct way. They teach as that throughout life we should always have and keep an open mind about things. The old saying "Practice what you preach" doesn't seem to mean anything to them.

The students of Dobbins seem to accept the younger teachers more than the ones who have been here for years. I know that the older teachers are supposed to know more and that experience is the key to success. But, the younger and fresher teachers don't have the experience although they have already won the confidence of the students at Dobbins. You may think they are too young to know and that they may not be able to control a class, but the teachers at Dobbins who can still feel that they have something to learn have a better chance of fulfilling their greatest expectations.

—By C.R.

Dear Mr. D.

Do you know the old tale about the tin man that had no oil and rusted. Well I feel principals of schools should teach at least one period a day. After they have been away from the classroom so long as you have their contact with the education of young people diminishes.

You walk around the halls without ever smiling. If I were principal of the greatest school in the country I would surely smile about it. You complain about noise in the auditorium, and, when the noise stops you complain about something else. In conclusion I wanted to tell you that we're only human beings.

Very Sincerely yours, A Concerned student (Concerned about you mostly)

The day before the term ended and the summer break started, the students who worked on their magazine brought the 325 to 350 copies to my classroom. They then handed out a copy to every teacher and counselor in the school. I felt the counselors should be involved so they might follow up with those students of mine whose writings suggested they might need some emotional support. I placed twelve copies of the magazine in my desk. As soon as my first class began, I told the students that they had done their job well, and no matter what might happen to me, it was my turn to do what I had to do and their responsibility was over. Almost immediately after I said this, I was paged over the classroom intercom to report to the principal's office. I went downstairs and met the principal in the hall. He was with the same teacher who initially gave me my class roll book. They were with a student of mine and the boy's father.

I had given all my student's a B for their final grade. However, for some reason this young boy had been singled out, and they had changed his English grade to a failing one and were now trying to convince the boy and his father that this was in the child's best interest. I told the father they had no right to do this and that they were being dishonest to his son. The father, overwhelmed, had little choice but to go along with the principal and the other teacher. None of my other students experienced this change of grade.

The principal now turned to me. With magazine in hand and finger on the short essay "How I View Homosexuality," he said, "We don't discuss things like this in school." I replied, "Where, then, do we discuss it? School is an appropriate place." I asked if he had read it. He said no and ordered me to collect the magazines from all the teachers. I refused, saying I had given my word to my students that the magazine would show the faculty what topics they valued as it impacted their lives. In addition, they appreciated the opportunity to express their thoughts in writing. He angrily replied, "You're fired; give me your keys," and handed them to the head of the English department while asking her to escort me out of the building. I indicated that I had a jacket in my room and I would like to get it. She opened the door to my classroom, and I went to my desk and, much to her chagrin, retrieved my copies of the magazine. I left the school thinking, I hope I accomplished something more than to force the school to become more careful of whom they hired in the future. I never imagined what was to follow.

5

THE REWARDS THAT HONOR A JOB WELL DONE

EARLY THE NEXT MORNING I received a phone call from the district office asking that I immediately report there. Apparently being fired had to be officially reviewed. I met with a woman who readily communicated her annoyance with me, and while being chastised, the phone rang. She asked if I had spoken to the *Philadelphia Bulletin*. I had not spoken to anyone, and at this point I left her office to obtain a copy of this newspaper. The *Philadelphia Bulletin* was the largest-circulation newspaper in Philadelphia, until it closed in 1982.

There on the front page was this headline: "Dobbins Teacher Axed over Pupil's Sex Essays." I was stunned and frightened as the title suggested that I had done something salacious. How could someone write an article about me without ever having spoken to me or read the class magazine? I had little choice but to go to the offices of the *Bulletin* with copies of the magazine, hoping to speak to the author of the unsigned article. Initially, I was asked to leave the building, but I refused and repeatedly demanded to speak with the individual who wrote this damning headline. Eventually, I was introduced to a woman who was the author and immediately gave her a copy of the magazine, asking her to read it while I waited. She did and then apologized, indicating that someone from the high school had phoned the information in (I never found out who this individual was and what their motive might have been). She added that she would print a retraction but could not promise when or where it might appear in the newspaper. It did appear about four days later in the obituary section.

My next and seemingly only option was to go to the office of the *Philadelphia Inquirer*, Philadelphia's second major newspaper. Almost immediately after entering and asking to speak with a reporter, I was greeted by Mr. John Corr and Miss Rose DeWolf, who said they had been trying to contact me as I was now a topic of the Associated Press. I was to learn that the Associated Press distributes news 24/7 across a thousand newspapers and their journalists. I gave both reporters their own copies of the magazine and asked them to read them before we spoke. When they were finished, both Mr. Corr and Miss DeWolf said they would help me in ways they were able. They did, and for one entire week they wrote supportive articles, many on the front page, and continued even after I was reinstated by the incoming superintendent of schools. During this week, I learned that the principal of Dobbins, after collecting copies of the magazine from those teachers who handed them over, burned them. In addition, I also became aware that many of my students and their parents picketed the administration building of the board of education in support of me. Excerpts from the magazine were repeated in newspapers throughout the United States. I eventually received a letter from Harvard University indicating that I had made one of the most significant contributions to education that year. The story and selections from the magazine also appeared in the *Saturday Review of Literature*.

I can never repay the debt I owe to Mr. Corr and Miss DeWolf for their personal support and the daily articles supporting what had really occurred at Dobbins. Their writings were characterized by intelligence and discrimination, which reflected their commitment to quality in public education for all social classes.

The Rewards That Honor a Job Well Done

I was eventually interviewed by a reporter from the *Philadelphia Tribune*—the oldest continuously published African American newspaper in the United States. The reporter, initially skeptical of my motives, spoke with me for a relatively long time, and eventually my picture along with the Dobbins story appeared on the front page of this newspaper.

After a week of newspaper articles, television interviews, and hearing myself spoken about endlessly on news radio, the following appeared in the media from the Office of Informational Services, Philadelphia Public Schools, by Dr. Mark Shedd, recently appointed superintendent of schools:

> There were a number of ambiguities surrounding the case of Mr. Harlem, as there are inevitably are in any disagreement. There is little doubt, for instance, that he handled himself less than wisely in his confrontation with the principal, Mr. D. But for all the cloudy circumstances, one fact stands out clearly: Mr. Harlem is a talented young man who was doing an interesting and first-rate job of teaching.
>
> He is the kind of teacher we must not only tolerate but encourage in the school system. He had the guts to take a few chances and venture onto rugged terrain in an effort to get students deeply involved in learning—in this case by developing in them an enthusiasm for self-expression through writing about subjects of relevance and concern to themselves. To the best of my knowledge, none of his superiors at Dobbins or other levels of the system deny this.
>
> Why then was he removed from his post?
> The real answer, I believe, is that the whole affair exemplifies one way in which the mechanics of a system can work at cross-purposes to the primary goals of the system. For, when a

bureaucracy becomes unwieldy—and, as I have said before, it is my feeling that the School District's bureaucracy has become unwieldy—its tolerance for the new, the unusual and the risky diminishes.

In the case of Mr. Harlem, a difficult decision was rendered under pressure of time. It was an understandable decision but, I believe, an unfortunate one. We can ill afford to discourage the quality of teacher Mr. Harlem represents by invoking uniform of rigid standards and procedures which tend to stifle creativity. It is the system which must yield when it gets in the way of the development of children, and not the individual teacher whose style conflicts with the system.

With regard to the topics of the magazine Mr. Harlem's class produced, it is true they were controversial—race, sex, politics, drug addiction, and so on. But a look at the magazine itself should convince anyone that they were treated circumspectly and, more importantly, with honesty. There is nothing in the magazine which could be considered salacious or immoral.

To take the attitude that young men and women should not be allowed to freely and honestly explore, in school, concerns which are pressing in their daily existence is to say that education bears no relationship to life. I reject this position completely. In fact, it seems to me that the widespread alienation of our youth today is primarily a result of a collapse of communication with the adult generation. Suppression of controversial student concerns merely serves to widen this gap. If, on the other hand, curriculum includes social issues of such concern to all of us, the schools, society, and youth will be well served. . . . It is my strong feeling that curriculum must be relevant to the lives and concerns of students even if it means getting into hot issues such as race, sex, politics or religion—some of the very topics Mr. Harlem's students treated.

Gamblers and mavericks must have a place in the system for they are so often the ones who come up with the new and better ideas. I am not sure, however, that you would call Mr. Harlem a gambler or a maverick. He was simply attempting the kind of teaching all good teachers do and more should try. I am not trying to brush aside the fact that Mr. Harlem lacked diplomacy. He disobeyed the order of a principal and in doing so his judgment and manner left much to be desired. For this he should be admonished. It seems to me that mature professionals should be able to negotiate their differences rationally and satisfactorily.

But I do not feel his diplomacy is the basic question. His teaching is. Therefore, I have asked that Mr. Harlem be reinstated. I hope he will consider education as a permanent career.

This reinstatement was printed in many newspapers throughout the United States. I subsequently received dozens of letters from teachers, former educators, and individuals praising the Dobbins episode. Surprisingly, I never received a single crank letter. Almost immediately, the school system's director of English curricula, Mrs. Marjorie Farmer, requested me for curriculum advice.

After the reinstatement I received a number of requests from radio talk programs to appear on their shows. I turned down all these requests because I strongly believe that when the war is over, one doesn't take prisoners. While the positive reaction to what happened was rewarding and very much appreciated, I have to mention two profoundly meaningful events that I remember as though they happened yesterday.

During the week following my dismissal, with the newspapers and radio constantly mentioning me and the Dobbins story, I received a phone call that radio and television reporters along with representatives from the teacher's union wanted to meet with me in front of the high school. When I became a long-term substitute, I had joined the teachers' union, but after being fired, they wanted no part of me because of the magazine's topics. I lived, at that time, on a second floor, and when I left early that morning, the steps outside my building were filled with twelve or more of my students. I asked why they were there, and they told me they knew, from the newspapers, that I was going through a difficult time and they simply wanted to see how I was. They'd had no idea when I would leave my apartment, but indicated they were prepared to wait. I explained that I had to go to the high school for an interview, and when I saw disappointment in their expressions, I said, "Let's all go together." We then formed a car train to Dobbins. There we met the reporters, cameramen, and union representatives. I was not alone.

The first question put to me by one union member was about my involvement with the students and parents picketing after my firing. I said, "Ask my students if you want the truth." One young girl spoke up, and I will never forget her reply. She said, "If it were not for Mr. Harlem I would not have never spoken up, and now I have the right and courage to face you and tell you he had nothing to do with the picketing. In fact, he told us it was now his responsibility to deal with the principal and we had done our job." Many of the other students gave the same message, and ultimately all questions were directed to the students. There are times in our lives that we feel validated and nothing but nothing can match these treasured moments when others touch us and move us so deeply.

The second event I will repeat now, out of sequence, but I feel it is necessary to illustrate that we can never fully measure the effect we have on other human beings. The reader may remember I had both eleventh- and twelfth-grade students. Fast-forward one year and I received a phone call from the head counselor, who asked if I wanted to see my eleventh-grade students graduate. I did, but I also realized my presence might embarrass the principal, so I declined the invitation. The counselor said I could sit in the balcony and not be seen. I agreed and watched the graduation. When it was over I started to leave, but the counselor said that my former students were in the gym waiting to see me. I went to the gym and was emotionally overwhelmed to see not only my students but their parents and family members, who had waited a year to meet and thank me for those all too few months I had been fortunate enough to be part of their child's life. To say that I was moved beyond words for this honor would be a gross understatement. However, to say it impacted and influenced my life's professional and personal behaviors would also be a gross understatement. An important point not to be glossed over is that parents, when they felt education had something to offer their child, responded on their own. How often are parents in the inner city blamed for not caring enough to become involved when we as educators have not earned their trust, their confidence, and communicated we truly care for their sons and daughters?

It was still June, and having been in the news for the better part of that month, I was asked by the school board to evaluate a special tutoring program for Philadelphia teachers who had been in the classroom for twelve to fifteen years but had been unable to pass the National Teacher Examination. Several hundred teachers qualified for this special program. Half the teachers would be tutored during the month of July, from 9:00 a.m. to noon, and paid ten dollars per hour along with coffee and doughnuts. The other half of the teachers would be in the August group. All instruction was geared toward taking and passing the National Teacher Examination. In fact, we were given an old copy of this exam to sharpen our test-taking skills. This program was funded by a federal grant, and I was asked to participate as any other teacher but required to provide an evaluation of the program at the end of July. I agreed on one condition: when the teachers took the actual exam at the end of July, I would have access to their scores so that

I might correlate their performances with the subjects they had been teaching during their career. Five days a week for three hours and thirty dollars each day, instructors who had passed the national examination provided tips, strategies, et cetera on how to take the test. At the end of the month I handed in my evaluation. One word: *worthless*. At first, the administrators of the program thought, Here goes Harlem again, until I showed them the data. Teachers who had been teaching English, for example, scored in the fifteenth percentile in their own subject area, and most of the results reflected the same lack of improvement. I pointed out that the majority would have performed better if they had been blindfolded and left their responses up to chance. They understood, and the August program was canceled. As far as I knew, these teachers were needed in the classroom and continued to teach.

September brought with it the awareness that I had to register for school without sufficient tuition and no specific program. One afternoon while wandering through the psychology building, a professor stopped me and asked what was bothering me. I had no idea who this gentleman was, but I asked outright if he had the time to listen to what had happened to me the semester before when I resigned from a flawed program. This gentleman listened, took my name, and said he would look into the facts I had presented and would get back to me. Within two days I heard from him and he suggested that I contact Dr. Robert Kleiner, chairman of the Department of Social Psychology, who was looking for research assistants. I met with Dr. Kleiner and explained my interests and background, and he suddenly asked if I was the teacher who had been in the newspapers. I answered and was immediately hired. I became the psychologist, along with two sociology and one communication major, doing research on a new treatment model for "backward patients" from the Philadelphia State Hospital. "Backward patients" meant those with significant mental illness who spent a large part of their lives in this particular mental institution. The patients I worked with had been in the hospital from twelve to fifty-two years. I remained a research assistant with Dr. Kleiner's innovative program until I finished my master's degree. Parenthetically, Dr. Kleiner's treatment was so effective, it was adopted as the primary model to treat severe mental patients in the country of Norway.

Because of the Dobbins notoriety, I was contacted by the director of the Columbia School, Mr. Charles Clisby, and asked if I would implement a values workshop at his school located in center city, Philadelphia. The Columbia School was a small, private facility for affluent male students. These adolescents had problems with drugs and alcohol and exhibited multiple manifestations of maladaptive behaviors. Dr. Kleiner gave me permission to teach at this school Tuesday and Thursday mornings. Each class was one hour, and I dealt with issues of personal and social responsibility, integrating an approach similar to the one I had used at Dobbins. Again, the emphasis was on how their behavior communicated what they were, and I explored what message they really wanted to send, reminding them you are what you do. I challenged their behaviors and justifications while personally accepting them and, at the same time, presented alternative values for their consideration. This left them open to listening and eventually accepting me.

One Thursday a student asked if he could bring in a guest speaker, Ira Einhorn. Mr. Einhorn was a recognized leader of the counterculture, anti-establishment, and anti-war movement of the 1960s and '70s. The following Tuesday Mr. Einhorn came to our class. I offered him my chair, which he rejected; instead, he sat down on the floor and proceeded to talk for the hour. His message essentially was, "Do your own thing, and the hell with rules and the establishment."

As I listened, and watched the expression on my students' faces, I tried to divine how they were reacting to this bearded, somewhat mesmerizing guru, feeling less secure in my own efforts. The following Tuesday my students' first response, without my having asked, was, "Einhorn had no right telling us that our behavior has no effect on others." They flatly rejected his pseudo philosophy. (Mr. Einhorn died in prison, April 2020, serving a life sentence for the murder of his girlfriend.)

One evening I received a phone call from one of my Columbia School students. He was in New York City and had been rolled, stripped of his money and clothes, by "hippies." I went to the city and brought this terrified sixteen-year-old back home. I met with his father, who told me he had tried to make a man of his son, in part by taking him to prostitutes. Needless to say, I forcefully explained that this was the worst possible thing, among others he had tried, "to force his son to become a man." I then realized I had to meet with the parents of these young men, and I did hold evening meetings to discuss the adolescents' perceptions of themselves, their world and strategies, and needs they still had in order to cope with this difficult stage of their lives. At some point the adults offered to pay me for what I had done and was doing at the school. I refused; after all, I was making twenty dollars a week from my teaching. Instead, the adults donated a library in my honor, and I could not have been more pleased. I have always loved books, and their gift was truly appreciated.

Because of the Dobbins experience, I was also asked to give lectures on how adults learn to read at the Philadelphia Adult Basic Education Academy, in West Philadelphia. One evening I received a phone call from a physics teacher at Olney High School in Philadelphia—a school my two brothers had attended. This teacher had read about Dobbins, and he was asking for a suggestion as his class was unmotivated and failing tests, and he had no idea what to do to remedy this situation. Physics is a difficult subject, and after questioning him, it appeared his tests were quite difficult with an inordinately high failure rate. I suggested that the next test be made so easy that it would be impossible for anyone to do poorly. This would be like adding a constant to the equation and would serve the purpose of motivating those students who probably felt there was no hope, so why try. He said he would take my suggestion and get back to me. Several weeks later I heard from him. The suggestion worked, and this dedicated teacher learned that teaching must consider the emotions as well as the intellect.

Shortly before the publicity from the Dobbins event slipped into the recent past, I received a phone call from a television producer who asked if I would meet at her home with a group of interested teachers to explain how I had accomplished what I had with my English students. I agreed, and when I was introduced to her guests I was startled. Several of the teachers in attendance were those I had briefly had in high school. They were wonderful teachers, but my junior year was during the time of Joseph McCarthy, and these men had been removed from Central High School because of possible Communist involvement. Joseph McCarthy, a demagogue, destroyed countless lives with unsubstantiated accusations and public attacks. Seven teachers were removed during my junior year. Without a doubt, they were the finest teachers I had during my years at Central. Eventually, Senator McCarthy was censured in 1955. This put an end to the era known as McCarthyism. Yet these teachers I was now facing were still interested in how we might improve teaching.

After I spoke that evening, the woman who had invited me asked if I might be interested in a television show of my own. I did go to the studio and was interviewed, but nothing came of it.

After finishing my master's degree, as previously mentioned, I worked for four and a half years at Temple University Hospital in Philadelphia in the rehabilitation and neurosurgical departments. These were wonderful years for me, but I was periodically reminded of Dobbins in various ways. One afternoon, I went into a bank; the teller was a former student whose essay still remains in the magazine *Introspection*.

As previously described, while at Temple Hospital, I worked with paralyzed young men. In Philadelphia, where the number of spinal cord injuries from gang war activities was appalling, I felt there would be multiple gains if these wheelchair students were permitted to return to the schools from which they came.

On one occasion I recommended a young quadriplegic patient of mine return to his high school in order to continue his education.

He and his classmates were overjoyed at the idea, and the school was initially receptive to the idea. However, a school counselor delayed the admission, claiming that "a cripple does not belong among normal students." I wondered, *Who is the cripple here?*

After leaving Temple Hospital, I attended the University of Pennsylvania for my PhD, and I was fortunate to become a teaching fellow. One of my responsibilities was to place counseling majors in school settings for their practicums. One student wanted to be placed in a high school, and off we went to Dobbins. The former vice principal, now the principal, was the gentleman who had initially brought the magazine to the principal's attention, resulting in my dismissal. I looked at him, and he knew what I was thinking. Without my saying a word, he said, "Can't a guy change his mind?"

One evening I received a phone call from a professor at the University of Massachusetts. He asked if I knew a young man whom he named. This was the former student of mine who had been considered a failure and had spoken to me about having a daughter. The professor wanted me to know that this now college graduate was encouraging youngsters in poverty areas to remain in school, and he began every lecture about his Dobbins experience and relationship with me. Needless to say, I was thrilled for this young man and overwhelmed by how he honored me.

While working on my dissertation, I was asked by St. Leonard's Academy, a Catholic school in West Philadelphia, to teach chemistry to twelfth-grade students and English to sixth graders. I did and loved being in the classroom where these students were more than kind to me.

After graduation, I was asked if I would develop a teaching program at Penn's Dental School, where they had developed a program to train "exceptional" (those with intellectual disabilities) female students to become dental aides. I was not responsible for course content but developed teaching strategies and techniques that I communicated to the instructors so as to maximize learning in their unique student population. The program was a success, and I was honored by the students asking me to speak at their graduation.

All these recognitions, while flattering, were also frustrating in that I realized, to effectively educate, there was the need for modifications in teaching strategies, teacher training, teacher selection, and equal educational opportunities for all regardless of race or socioeconomic status.

My dissertation involved training fifty-nine learning-impaired students in the first, second, and third grades how to increase their attention and concentration in order to facilitate not only learning but to help with voluntary self-regulation of undesirable behaviors. The students were 100 percent African American and were considered among the lowest-achieving students in the city of Philadelphia. Pre- and post-test measures were employed with the experimental and control groups. Outcome measures of this study clearly revealed that the attention-trained group exhibited dramatic increases in attention, concentration, memory, cognitive mediation, and flexibility to task demands as evidenced by more productive task approaches than students in the control group. Treatment gains did not dissipate but were maintained over time.[27]

I would train ten students at a time in an empty classroom, where I needed quiet time. However, a teacher in the adjacent classroom would always be screaming, and one day I went into her classroom, where there was a young third-grade girl standing and crying as she was being berated by this teacher in front of the class. I asked the teacher to stop and told her how inappropriate, harmful, and disruptive her behavior was. This teacher knew me and said, "Steve, when I was in college, I was taught children did not have feelings until age twelve." This is a true story; said by a tenured teacher.

One of my research assistants involved with the above study, for her doctoral dissertation, wanted to see how my results translated into the classroom. She took thirty-five of the school-labeled "poorest readers" in the first-, second-, and fourth-grade classes in the same school and trained the students using the same attention-training technique. This was a controlled study with a group who did not receive the attention training compared with the group that did. The reading measures used were the same as those used by the Philadelphia school system. After training, no contact was made with the students for thirty days. After this period, the research assistants returned and administered retests. The results clearly showed that the attention-trained students demonstrated increased self-control, flexibility of thought, attention, concentration, and problem-solving skills. Word recognition had improved to the extent that this group had, on their own, increased their reading from one- to three-year levels. No such gains or behavior changes were found in the control group, who had not received the training.

The teachers who were encouraged to be part of the entire study never recognized the changes in the trained students. The tragedy is that once these children were labeled, no effort was made to teach them or expect they could learn. Despite the gains made by the students themselves, we found they were reading the same books they had been given the month before the training began. The teachers were not remotely aware that these pupils had increased their reading levels. Once trained in how to increase their attention and concentration, the technique strengthened itself and did not require our follow-up. However, in a better situation, it could have been utilized and therefore reinforced by their teachers.[27]

A principal from an elementary school in the Germantown section of Philadelphia heard about my attention training program and contacted me, asking if I had something to offer her school. My assertion is that when a pupil starts school, he or she is given pencils and papers, et cetera, but *they are not taught how to pay attention.* When I was in school and a teacher said, "Pay attention!" it meant fold your hands on the desk, look ahead, and be quiet. Yet my mind could continue to wander in any direction. I began training every student in this school, from kindergarten through the sixth grade, including a class for autistic youngsters. Each class would come into the library for ten minutes each day for a total of ten days. Their teachers were also trained in how to use the technique. After training, if a teacher wanted her students to focus and attend to her instruction, all she had to do was say, "You know what to do," and the students demonstrated voluntary and increased focus. Learning was significantly increased as reported back to me from this principal, who encouraged me to present the results and the approach to the administrators at the board of education.

I did as suggested; this is what transpired. I explained that I had a valid attention-training program that cost nothing. They were free to check with the principals of two schools as to the efficacy of the program, and they did. Eventually I was told that the program would be too expensive. I reiterated that it cost nothing as no supplies were involved, simply teacher instruction in their respective schools. Their position was that if it worked, as I had indicated, every teacher would want it, and this was where the expense would come in. To this day, I remain amazed at this mindless attitude that would deny students and teachers alike a strategy to facilitate learning in a pleasant, voluntary, self-controlled, and successful environment. The entire program is included in the appendix and will be mentioned again in chapter 6.

After one year at the Dental School, I began work as a clinical/neuropsychologist in several area hospitals. In addition, I am also a licensed school psychologist and would often lecture to both Philadelphia school psychologists and vocational counselors for the state Office of Vocational Rehabilitation. I became interested in preventing the incidence of teen pregnancy, which at that time was a significant problem. I encouraged the development and promotion of two thin booklets, almost in a comic-book format, titled, "Ten Heavy Facts about Sex" and "Protect Yourself from Becoming an Unwanted Parent." I was called to one of the school administration centers and shown a closet full of these booklets. Two days later, I received a phone call telling me the booklets had been destroyed because I was promoting genocide of the black race. I never found out who made this decision that ultimately would exacerbate unnecessary harm by denying students' knowledge of the basic facts of life.

Shortly after this I was asked by the new superintendent of schools to attend a meeting at the Octavius Cato School in Philadelphia. They wanted my opinion as to whether it was a reasonable idea to combine the Cato with the Daniel Boone school. Both of these were remedial disciplinary schools, where "incorrigible students" were placed. (The Boone school closed in 2012.) I toured the Cato school's classrooms, spoke with and observed many students, and toured the vocational training classrooms. One example should suffice of those issues that influenced my report to the superintendent. The shoe repair workshop was most impressive; large, airy, and full of equipment and supplies necessary to repair and probably even make shoes. I watched the students and was shocked to see them not working on shoes but making key rings, while the teacher simply sat in a chair doing nothing. These were simply small oval pieces of leather with a hole punched in one end.

As I toured the classes, I saw several students with obvious head injuries. The location of the injury permitted an educated guess of their behavior. When I spoke to the teachers about particular students and what I felt their behavior might be, the teachers invariably asked me how I knew this. After my tour I suggested it might be a mistake to combine the two schools, at least until Cato had improved its programs and teacher education in a number of critical areas. The schools were not, at that time, combined.

Because of Dobbins and my additional involvement with the Philadelphia school system, I was asked to participate as a school psychologist in a new alternative program, the Alternative Placement Center North. This was a small high school, funded by the federal government, where the most difficult and recalcitrant students were assigned and bused, the goal being a program with small classes permitting individual instruction and psychological testing.

I was a consultant to this program for fourteen years and did extensive psychological testing on 1,400 individual students. The vast majority of these students were normal and decent adolescents, some of whom had experienced early life disruption of basic needs, including stimulus deprivation. Many continued to lack emotional support, encouragement, and the understanding adolescents often require. In addition, some had not received adequate medical care, and I was fortunate to recommend quite a few for diabetic/medical evaluations when I was convinced a health issue played a role in their adjustment and learning difficulties. There were some who had intellectual deficits and would have benefited from a less academically oriented program, and I identified a few who had significant sociopathic tendencies. I would always bring my findings to the school counselors and principal.

One of the major weaknesses of the program resulted from the frequent change of principals and the weakness of some of the staff. One teacher was an alcoholic and would often ask me to take his classes as he was actually too sick to teach. One of the counselors, a relatively young woman, I felt was suicidal. I brought this to the attention of the principal, who dismissed my opinion until the day of this counselor's funeral.

The goals of this program were correct, but what was lacking was appropriate staff training and an understanding of students' lives and present needs. Having failed in their previous schools, was it reasonable to expect them to blossom because the school was smaller? There was now an absence of anything but several academic subjects. No sports, no art, no music, no ability for self-expression, but only the expectation to behave in class and do their work. There was no opportunity for self-discovery and a lack of communication of the dignity and worth of each and every student. There was no attempt to build self-pride in one's accomplishment. A grade of A or B simply does not do this as this has little or no carryover. There were kind and sympathetic teachers and administrators during my fourteen years at this program. However, the educational model they followed was simply to repeat the same teaching strategies that had brought the students to this program in the first place. Without this recognition and acceptance of the individual's uniqueness, it was unreasonable to expect different teaching outcomes.

Chapter 6 will introduce some reasonable and, I believe, necessary changes in pedagogy and teacher training that will hopefully enable us to fulfill the promise we repeatedly made so very many years ago. That is, equal educational opportunity for every one of our youngest citizens in the United States.

6

THOUGHTS ON RECONSTRUCTING OUR EDUCATIONAL SYSTEM

I REALIZE THE EDUCATION MODEL THAT WE, as a nation, are used to will take time to return due to the impact of COVID-19. However, as I mentioned previously, I do believe it will return to the familiar and recognizable model we have used, even with some technological changes.

When we speak of equal opportunity it is imperative to eliminate the distinctions and perpetuation of inequalities across lines of race, ethnicity, and class. Presently we seem to have two systems of public education. One system is based in the suburbs and in the wealthier urban districts of our country. When compared to the achievement of students with those of our international peers we, even here, are not doing an adequate job. Public education even in the suburban or more affluent areas is often unsatisfactory.

The other system of public education, based primarily in poorer urban areas, is failing its students. This is evidenced by high dropout rates, and many that graduate have diplomas that are not indicative of adequacy in basic subject areas. Many are unprepared for the world of work, higher education, or advanced technical training. This situation creates not only unemployment, poverty, crime, and civil disorder but also a multiplicity of social problems. Attempting to alleviate these problems with minimum-wage laws, welfare payments, urban renewal, and increased policing has been shown to create other problems. The most carefully designed corrective social measures will continue to fail and will not change the fact that we are leaving a substantial portion of Americans behind unless there is dramatic public education reform.

The overall purpose of this chapter is to prepare students to engage in the world around them and to lead happy, healthy lives in which they are the authors of their own self-determined successes. To do this, we must, as much as is possible, convey appropriate academic content, develop skills, cultivate confidence, and engender good judgment. This facilitates students' capacity to understand themselves and others.

The suggestions that follow are designed to recognize first the role that cultural anthropology has always played in children's educational development. We have traditionally ignored this role while developing our educational philosophies and programs. For example, many of the games Roman children played two thousand years ago continued to be played through the ages and up to the present. For thousands of years children have played with sling shots, yo-yos, and marbles and games such as Kick the Can, hide-and-seek, and tic-tac-toe played the exact same way as today. How were the rules to these games communicated? Rules were not written down but passed on nonverbally through the interactions of young children.[28] It is precisely this interaction that early stimulation and education programs must capitalize upon and foster as part of any educational program in neighborhoods and communities, as we are inherently social beings. A child with the ability to play will communicate his or her knowledge, thereby increasing social development and even intellectual stimulation to their peers. The worth of appropriate interactional play between children in neighborhoods cannot be overstated. Today, this includes texting, competitive video games, and the multiple uses of computers.

Parental involvement in their child's education is of paramount importance. This has always been a recognized goal of most educational programs. The reader may recall that I tested 1,400 students at the Alternative Placement Center North. For the vast majority of these adolescents, **if I had one and only one magic recommendation, it would have been increased parental involvement early in their lives.**

While I was completing my dissertation in the school described in the previous chapter, I also had the opportunity to administer a $65,000 grant whose purpose was to increase parental interest in their child's classroom. I was permitted to pay each parent twenty dollars cash an hour, up to two hours each week, just to observe their son or daughter in class. The money was tax free and had no effect on any financial assistance the parent may have been receiving. I paid out only twenty dollars of the total amount of the grant, and the rest was returned to the funding source. Obviously, money is not the answer. I believe that most of these parents were interested in their children but were intimidated by their perceptions of the school or embarrassed by their own lack of education and simply not knowing what to expect. The communication that parents are necessary to and valued in their child's education must be established very early in a child's life. This is essential in the poorest urban areas if we are sincere about public education reform.

A child's preparation for learning and eventual participation in the world begins at birth and even before. I am suggesting that what I choose to call Play Care programs be established strategically throughout the poorest urban poverty pockets. These differ from day care and early childhood education programs. Through federal and/or state funding, these free programs would be established approximately every half mile in the poorest neighborhoods to encourage those pregnant or new parents and/or primary caregivers to walk in with their infant to take advantage of one of the Play Care centers. There will be parents who will not take advantage of this program. However, I am counting on those children who are exposed to this very early stimulation to ultimately interact in their homes and neighborhoods with those children who are not exposed to Play Care. Essentially these eventual neighborhood interactions will be stimulating and enrich their peer's development, much like the communication of children's games over the centuries. Play Care establishes the early foundations of social interactions and future learning.

A major focus of these centers is to not only help establish a strong bond between parent and child but help prepare the infant during its first year of rapid development to take advantage of the educational programs that are to follow. A new parent may feel the child is a disruption in their life, and it may help by having an empathetic instructor along with peers to offer support. These programs are essentially teaching and support focused with an emphasis on encouraging and teaching prospective parents and new parents how vital it is to become actively involved throughout their child's educational career. Infancy is just the beginning, and parents must have the courage to sustain this initial interest and not hesitate to hold teachers and administrators responsible for what and how is being taught to their children. I have often said to a parent, "If you purchased a hamburger for two dollars and it was visibly rotten, what would you do?" I then added, "What you did with this two-dollar hamburger, you are obligated to do for your child's education. That is, demand the best possible education by becoming actively involved with your child's school."

Play Care instructors will be college graduates who have received degrees in human/child development. They will be expected to explain to new parents the changing behaviors and capacities of the developing child throughout the first year of life; how to manage crying and feeding and the need and ways to nurture and teach through speaking, singing, play, and reading during this critical period of development. A talented instructor should have the ability to inspire individuals to be creative with their child, not to feel guilty when a child cries, and how to manage infant, as well as their own, fatigue and frustrations. Instructors should know when it is advisable to refer to a health-care professional for perceived developmental concerns.

Each Play Care facility should be painted in primary colors, and there should be soft music in the background along with mobiles and other appropriate stimuli for infants. Music is essential in the development of neuroplasticity in the brain. Full-spectrum lighting is obligatory as typical classroom fluorescent lights have repeatedly been shown to cause or exacerbate stress, anxiety, hyperactivity, and attention problems in many learners. **Full-spectrum lighting should be considered for all classrooms in our country**. It is naïve not to acknowledge that our external environment influences our behavior.[29]

Parents are free to drop into the centers without enrolling and without obligation, but are responsible for the feeding and care of their children. Sleeping infants will be held or placed in their strollers. Changing rooms will be available. Since infants' capacities change as they develop, the instructors will illuminate the emerging needs and blossoming capacities. As other parents observe these changes, it will help them understand their own child's development. Hopefully, it will be emphasized that playing with one's child at home build bonds and teaches the child that he or she is valued. Quality time, whether it is listening to music, reading a story, taking a walk together, or singing, builds a level of self-esteem in a child that lasts a lifetime. If one is a single parent or has only one child, invite family and friends over to share in these activities. It is never too early to start in a child's life. Involved parents are essential to a child's development throughout his or her formative years. Speaking to your infant even though she or he might not understand builds an everlasting relationship and sets the stage for the child's own language development.

Another goal of these centers is **to help establish a strong support system for parents in their communities that facilitates a communication of caring**. This places a large responsibility on each instructor, who will also develop the specifics of the programs. There also will be one supervising individual who meets with each instructor individually and in groups to evaluate their respective programs, encourage input, and make changes where and when advisable. The instructors should be reimbursed at a level commensurate with their education and responsibility. The Play Care model at this time should be seen as a pilot program, and its initial merits should be evaluated after one year through parents' opinions of their experiences. A true evaluation is only possible with a long-term follow-up program as children play with others in their neighborhoods.

One major problem I see with the programs that follow Play Care is that there are tremendous variations in day care and early-education programs. Educational requirements for teachers vary tremendously, accountability is often lacking, teacher training and certification is not uniform, and these programs have tremendous inconsistency in preparing children to benefit from public education in the elementary and junior high schools. These early programs, which are so critical, require the most talented and highly educated teaching staff. Unless we are prepared to implement this as a mandatory requirement, then nothing will change in these youngsters' future. If one doubts this, one simply has to look at the academic achievement of students of color and impoverished backgrounds. Day-care programs, while permitting a parent to work, are much more than babysitting resources. The stimulation that should be given to every child is of paramount importance during this critical period of development.

I also found that what is neglected in a large percentage of preschool programs and early-elementary grades is the awareness that children's play benefits the development of the whole child across social, cognitive, physical, and emotional domains. The American Academy of Pediatrics named play a central component in developmentally appropriate educational practices.

Under pressure of rising academic standards, play is being replaced by test preparation in kindergartens and grade schools, and parents whose goal is to give their preschoolers an academic advantage are led to believe that flash cards and educational toys will facilitate success. We have created a false dichotomy between play and learning. Scientific research has demonstrated that play is learning. Through play, children learn to regulate their behavior, learn to deal and cope with social relationships, and develop creativity. Play provides children with the opportunity to exert control over their situation, and play with peers provides the context that benefits not only the cognitive but the social and emotional development as well. From a child's perspective, the power in relationships typically belongs to the adults, but play permits children to control their own behaviors through negotiation with their peers.[30] A wonderful spinoff from play is that it also allows the parent to view the world through the eyes of a child once again.

It is beyond the scope of this book to review all preschool and elementary school programs, but I feel there are several points that should be stressed. One piece of advice gleaned from many years of clinical practice with children's learning problems is that when starting kindergarten or other early grades, a child is much better off being one of the older pupils in the class rather than one of the youngest. A young child's emotional and physical development often lags behind their cognitive. Development specialists have repeatedly found that many school problems, in learning and behavior, are related to this discrepancy. Giving extra time before starting kindergarten or first grade provides time for normal maturation and growth. Age cutoffs vary with school district policies throughout the United States, but being one of the older students in a particular age group is decidedly to that student's advantage. This recommendation must be explained to parents prior to their child's placement. A parent armed with this information is better prepared to evaluate the school's placement recommendation, which may or may not be to their child's advantage.

Teacher preparation will be discussed later in this chapter. However, the recommended qualifications for the selection and training of teachers made for the secondary education staff are strongly recommended for those who will be responsible for students in the elementary years as well. There are many very good programs throughout the United States whose achievements the reader can evaluate. I feel there are certain academic subjects that are essential to future academic success and personal growth and must be emphasized in both elementary, middle, and junior high school classrooms. These subjects are particularly relevant if we are to provide equality and success in public education. The suggestions that follow are for the majority of students who will enter the elementary grades. I recognize there will be youngsters who will be described as falling within the developmental-disabilities spectrum, but the suggestions presented can be adjusted to maximize the achievements of many of these exceptional pupils. Here is where parental education and involvement is most essential as schools tend to provide supplemental or remedial services that are the least expensive and easiest for them to implement, but not always in the best interest of the child.

Starting in kindergarten or first grade at the latest, I suggest classroom teachers consider training their youngsters how to focus their attention. As previously mentioned, we cannot expect children in these age groups to immediately attend because we say, "Class, pay attention." Based upon repeated research and the application of attention training in public schools, the efficacy of this training has been demonstrated to be a potent learning aid. Again, included in the appendix is a detailed training manual the purpose of which is to guide the teacher in the application of this procedure with their students. In this respect, this is no different than selecting a particular method for teaching spelling, for example. In this case, the goal of attention training is to impart to each child the ability to develop internal controls enabling them to demonstrate increased capacities for attention, concentration, memory, and cognitive mediation. This skill then can be utilized by each student and teacher throughout their remaining school years. It is also suggested that every effort be made to bring the parents into the classroom at some point to observe the impact of and learn the training procedure while being encouraged to consider it in the home. The efficacy of attention training as outlined should be evaluated in both the home as well as the school.

For disadvantaged students, the next eight years are critical. If particular educational goals are not achieved by the start of high school, then the next four years are pointless. Talented teachers are essential to these elementary and junior high school years. Teachers must resist following a lockstep curriculum, with its mandatory testing, and concentrate on several indispensable goals until the majority of students have achieved them to the best of their abilities.

The rudiments of reading and writing begin in kindergarten through the teacher's reading literature commensurate with the child's age. Please do not forget the necessary role that play contributes to the learning process. However, during the following years, disadvantaged students *must* be taught to write meaningful sentences and paragraphs that readers can easily understand. Writing skills are an essential element of communication that permits an individual to express their opinions, thoughts, and ideas effectively. If students do not demonstrate strong writing skills by the eighth grade, then the schools have failed them and severely limited an individual's potential to benefit from additional education and ultimately experience success in the work force. Standardized group testing is not indicative of an individual's skill attainment. Each student must be evaluated individually, and teaching tailored to each pupil's level of progress. Higher-achieving students can also be asked to tutor their peers along with their teacher's support.

I cannot overemphasize the need for a child to master reading. We live in an information age, and learning to read is more important than ever. Whether it is comic books, regular books, magazines, or e-books, reading cements a child's language skills. Reading helps a child further develop their vocabulary in a way that everyday conversation cannot. Even when a young pupil does not understand everything they read, they are able to come to conclusions about new words from the context of material.

Reading is especially necessary with today's technology. One cannot gather information from the Web or communicate via email and social media unless one can read and write. Being well read is a positive attribute in society as it suggests increased intelligence. Parents must be encouraged, if possible, to read to their youngster; this builds a relationship with the parent and with reading itself. Books often permit us to travel to places we may never otherwise visit or have even known about;

thus, reading opens the world. Please, when selecting literature to read, do not forget to let students select literature of their times with which they can more readily identify. Without this focus on the achievement of strong reading and writing skills, nothing will have been done to correct the inequities in public education for the disadvantaged student.

There will be students who exhibit difficulties with reading and writing, and these problems must be identified at the earliest possible ages. Special support must be provided to these pupils by teachers who are knowledgeable in current research as well as remedial strategies. Parents should be encouraged to supplement the teaching of their child at home. Talented and knowledgeable teachers adjust their teaching goals where and when necessary to meet individual needs. For example, my younger brothers and I are products of the Philadelphia public school system. When we were in school there was no such thing as a learning-disability classroom. Teachers adjusted their teaching styles for those who had difficulties with particular subject areas. My brother never learned to express himself in writing, yet he excelled in science and became an outstanding pharmacist. His teachers never labeled him nor treated him as though he was deficient. He simply was unable to express himself through writing. Many years later I believed his ambidexterity probably contributed to his writing difficulty.

That there are shortcomings and fear in the discipline of mathematics seems to be understood by everyone. Yet with proper instruction, this subject, the cradle of all creations, can be understood during the formative periods of a student's education. Everyone—be it a cook, a carpenter, a mechanic, a chemist, a musician—uses mathematics in their everyday life. Pupils should be taught to employ concrete applications related to their everyday lives and also be encouraged to think about their own additional daily applications of this subject. There are STEM programs for those interested in increasing their skills in math, science, computer programming, and other related twenty-first-century activities. There are wonderful books about the role math plays in our lives that might be integrated into the reading curriculum. Computer instruction is recognized as being essential in the teaching-learning equation throughout the twelve school years, but as Rabindranath Tagore reminds us, "the best textbook for the pupil is the teacher."[6]

In addition, I hope that music is utilized, not as a separate class but by being integrated into math, reading, and even writing instruction. So many schools have eliminated music and art, as though it has less relevance to a student's life. Nothing could be further from the truth. A creative and innovative teacher should be able to weave all subjects into a connective mosaic.

For example, the study of history is essential as it allows one to make sense of the current world. And as we have seen in the earliest chapters, the history of educational goals has not been realized. Teaching history honestly will require talented, informed, and courageous teachers. For example, it is imperative that the present experiences of black Americans are seen not simply as the legacy of slavery and racism but as a deliberate continuation of restrictions on mobility. Systemic racism continues; as does white supremacy. An honest reading of Reconstruction and its consequences is vital to the understanding of the present. One interesting book, *The Negro Motorist Green Book*, a travel guide used by black families to travel somewhat safely in the Jim Crow era, makes for a good historical overview of another time period. Black students can take pride in reading about Rosa Parks's bus boycott in Montgomery, Alabama. The list of honest readings of black history is endless.

The talented teacher must deal with not only the historical record but the emotional reactions elicited by the facts. Students must be given free rein to express their opinions and solutions as they did in Dobbins. However, today there is a seriousness and an awareness that is glaring and screams for constructive change. One example, and there are many, is the unjust treatment of black Americans by authorities and the fear of law enforcement. The killing of George Floyd on May 25, 2020, has rocked this country and hopefully will force a discussion leading to long-overdue changes.

STEVEN HARLEM, P.h.D.

I would advise against a single history book, but rather encourage teaching by using various paperback publications and integrating the way the past has influenced and often determined the present. An understanding of the Civil Rights movement and the evolution of our constitution are but two examples. Memorizing names and dates for their own sake is not learning. Students' reading and writing about their own understanding of historical events and their impact on our present civilization is infinitely more valuable and indicative of real learning. History is best taught if the student is made aware of the connections between past and present events.

Hopefully, the talented teacher will also weave some art education into their instruction. A trip to the art museum and discussion about the history and evolution of perspective in art can level the playing field between children from financially challenged backgrounds and children who have had enrichment experiences. I understand that the No Child Left Behind mantra, with its pressure to raise test scores, has reduced classroom time devoted to the arts, science, and social studies. Who are these test scores really for? It is apparent, from the academic outcomes in the poverty-pocket schools, they are not for the students. This omission or elimination of art and music actually works against the improvements wanted in reading and math. Researchers have found that after experiencing exposure to art and music curricula, students scored higher on a standardized IQ test.[31] Art and music as well as history must be incorporated into all core classes along with education in sexuality. This should be self-evident to all dedicated educators.

Administrators in school programs that are forced to eliminate programs due to reductions in funding must rail against this as it only brings diminishing returns for individuals' lives and perpetuates deprivation and impoverishment.

Athletic programs must not be neglected. In addition to the more traditional sports, exposure to lacrosse, golf, tennis, field hockey, and other sports and various clubs not normally offered in the underserved communities, starting in the middle school and junior high and continued in the high school years, is, I feel, essential in an unbiased and balanced education. It not only broadens student experiences but gives life to latent talents and puts them on an even playing field with those more privileged.

I can think of no reason that a student should spend the next four years in essentially a repeat of the previous eight years. If reading and writing have not been demonstrably mastered, the next four years will not change this. Adolescent boredom coupled with a lack of meaning for their lives and an inability to meet their financial needs serves to increase the dropout rate, truancy, apathy, and acting out. I therefore propose that after the first two years of high school, students be encouraged to participate in a year away from school in a work-study program in which they will also receive a financial stipend. The money will be the responsibility of the respective board of education and possibly shared with the internship placement. When students first enter this new high school every detail of this program should be explained to them. Students who elect to spend their junior year in a work-study program and return for their senior year will still graduate after four years.

Academically, the skills, talents, and interests acquired in middle school and junior high will be refined and expanded upon during these first two years of high school. Investment banking, what constitutes adequate nutrition, and interviewing strategies are just a few of the additional curricula suggested. A continuing emphasis on writing must be maintained. It must also be explained that their achievement and interests will be followed during their freshman and sophomore years so that when the junior year arrives they have earned the right to participate in the work-study program. Reasonable academic and classroom performance during the first two years will increase the probability that a student will be satisfied with their work-placement choice. However, no decision is immutable; it can be modified or changed until the student is content with their choice. Vocational counselors are essential to obtaining placements and in helping students select from the thousands of possible vocations to spend the work year. One only has to look at the SCA Directory of Occupations (published by the US government) to view the thousands of existing occupations. Every work-study choice, ranging from truck driving to the study of law, must be treated with equal respect, encouragement, and support.

During the first two years, the students will also be offered electives in science, foreign language, music and art, writing, and computer and information technology (IT) training. Participation in sports for both men and women continues as in other high schools. Additionally, value workshops, akin to that described in my Dobbins experience, should be woven into the curriculum and conducted by sensitive and empathetic teachers. Cognitive as well as emotional development is advanced through affective education. Some of the most important questions we ask about our lives include "What should I believe? What should I want for myself and those I care about?" and "What should I do with my life." And as I previously mentioned, "What kind of person do I want to be?" Values exercises help one ask and answer these questions. Values exercises should begin in the elementary years to prepare the students to reflect on the above questions.

This program mirrors college, yet it also prepares students for success who elect another path. It does, however, communicate respect for and trust in the student. The counselors will follow their students in their placement to ensure that the students and the employers are mutually satisfied. Students are not obligated to participate in this program and may elect to spend all four years in the high school.

Once a student returns from his or her vocational placement year, they will not only return to classes but might also be considered to mentor younger students and even function as a teaching assistant. This helps change the atmosphere of the school and also sends a message into the neighborhood about the value and potential benefits of an honest education. The returning seniors can be viewed as role models for incoming freshmen and sophomores. If there is a realistic communication of hope based on staying in and being committed to school, then there may also be a reduction in multiple forms of social deviance and violence.

No matter how well conceptualized an educational program is, its success ultimately depends on talent, the competency and commitment of its teachers and administrators. This is true in every classroom throughout our country. Tragically, research demonstrates that teacher training in this country is inadequate. We continue to place the least experienced teachers in classrooms needing the best instruction. Many newly trained teachers too often lack the fundamental training in literacy needed to even have a chance at being effective teachers. There are omissions in instruction in the science of learning and a lack of awareness and interest in current educational research. This lack of teacher preparation will only perpetuate educational inequality. How did this happen in the United States?

Normal schools were established quite early in our history (1839) to train elementary school teachers for public schools. Initially called "normal schools" after the French phrase *ecole normale*, they were intended to establish a norm after which all other schools would be modeled.[32] Teachers were offered a two-year course beyond secondary education. In the twentieth century teacher-training requirements were extended to a minimum of four years, and by the 1930s most public normal schools had evolved into teachers' colleges. In the 1950s they had become departments or schools of education within universities. This assimilation of the normal school parallels the halting elevation of teaching to the status of a profession. By the end of the twentieth century, licensing requirements had stiffened considerably in public education, and salary increases and advancement often depended on the earning of advanced degrees and professional development. However, these incentives have promoted some undesirable behaviors. Some teachers take online courses that they may or may not actually complete themselves, and it is now possible to purchase online advanced degrees.

A study from the National Council on Teacher Quality states, "New teachers deserve training that will enable them to walk into their own classroom on their first day ready to teach." The report continues, "The problem is worse than we thought." The data shows that the academic caliber of many incoming students is quite low, and what they are taught often has little relevance to what they need to succeed in the classroom. Very few schools meet even a minimum standard of quality when it comes to using the best practices for educating teachers. "A large majority of programs (71%) are not providing elementary teacher candidates with practical research-based training in reading instruction methods that could reduce the current rate of reading failure. In the mathematics training of elementary teacher candidates, few programs emulate the practices of higher-performing nations such as Singapore or South Korea. Almost all programs (93%) fail to ensure a high quality of student teaching experience, where candidates are assigned only to highly skilled teachers and must receive frequent concrete feedback." Additional and significant omissions include the failure of many programs to provide teacher candidates with concrete classroom management strategies to improve classroom behavior problems as well as a failure to provide adequate content preparation for teachers in the subjects they will teach.[33]

I realize that creative, innovative, and courageous teachers are needed to go against prevailing dogma. Where will these teachers and administrators come from?

I am suggesting a return to the normal school model, as in Finland and France as well as other countries which have far superior teacher training programs. In these countries, teaching is a top-level profession, attracting the very best undergraduate students, putting them through a tough curriculum, and testing their capabilities. This is not true for US programs that are in the main mediocre. It is recognized that these programs can still produce good teachers, but the odds of success seem unfortunately low.

It is time to remove teacher training from the college and university undergraduate programs and establish separate professional programs to train teachers that raise the status of the profession to that of other professionals. Undergraduate instructors are frequently the least qualified to teach teacher candidates. They are often teaching assistants, and those that are "professors" have no formal experience as public school teachers and have not been trained to teach. This suggested professional teaching school, like medical and law schools, would be associated with a university.

Building on certain aspects of Finland's model for teacher and principal training, we have to begin with the most talented and motivated students. Recruitment for teacher candidates must begin with admitting to this new professional school from the top quartile of the college-bound cohort. Extracurricular activities and their score on a matriculation exam (one of this new school's own design) and observation in a teaching-like activity (our creation) will be also be considered before an applicant is admitted. This new professional school is, in addition to its emphasis on teacher training, a rich four-year college curriculum.

Primary school teachers will be required to minor in two primary-school curriculum subject areas in addition to majoring in multiple aspects of education. Secondary school teachers are required to major in the subject area they are to teach and complete a fifth year of education resulting in a master's degree. Teacher education is heavily research-based with a strong emphasis on pedagogical content.

Those teachers that teach the teacher candidates will, themselves, have to undergo a rigorous training program and have acquired at the minimum a master's degree. The completion of a master's degree is encouraged for all teachers, at which time the new teacher will receive state certification without taking the National Teacher Examination. Preschool teachers will have to have a bachelor's degree at the least if they are to be licensed.

Teachers, once in their classrooms, are autonomous, trusted professionals with a great deal of professional freedom and opportunities to decide their own teaching methods, materials, and student assessment. They can, with other teachers, suggest educational reform at the state and national levels along with new initiatives in teaching. Student difficulties with reading and writing are diagnosed at an early age, and special support is provided to pupils. All teachers will have to participate in continuing education.

Principals will be required to have teaching qualifications and to have taught a class at the level of the school they will lead. They will also be required to complete a program of educational leadership with practicums and to work, even part time, toward the attainment of a doctorate. The role of the principal, in addition to administrative duties, is to collaborate with the teachers for the purpose of increasing teaching outcomes. Ideally, school principals should continue to teach one class in their respective schools.

If the teaching profession is to become, once again, a highly respected profession, comparable to an engineer, lawyer, or medical doctor, then significant changes must occur now. I realize this represents significant changes in thinking and recruitment for existing university education programs. We are a large country and need many teachers to teach the fifty-five million public school students. I realize my proposed model will also present financial problems for universities and state funding streams. This problem is exacerbated by the new professional teacher being reimbursed at a much higher salary and one commensurate with their degree and skills. I understand any significant change may take time, but it must start now if we are to mend a festering wound that is horrifying in its consequences for those students who in the main have been cheated and ignored.

In addition, I propose that those teachers who work in schools where violence is commonplace be given a paid six-month respite after two years, much as we offer the combat soldier a break after his or her combat tour is completed. Maternal and paternal leave will also be covered. I encourage the recruitment of qualified teachers of color as they have the ability to more easily and understandably function as role models and encourage parental involvement in their child's school career.

Thoughts on Reconstructing Our Educational System

Elementary and high school counselors should receive a focused education after being selected with the same high standards as the prospective teaching candidates. Counselor education must encompass rigorous training in classroom management, student development through the age ranges, individual and group dynamics, and support strategies for the personal and social concerns of both students and teachers. Counseling certificates and placement can occur after a rigorous one-year internship. Continuing education requirements are mandatory for teachers as well as counselors.

I have attempted to make a case for the need to select the very strongest candidates as teachers. More than all the other professionals combined, teachers have the greatest impact on a child's life next to a parent. Their acting in loco parentis applies more than ever to the African American population in the areas of diet, exercise, absence of smoking, and overall physical health. Education by talented and knowledgeable teachers, through instruction on proper nutrition and exercise, can help reduce a high death rate from cardiovascular disease, diabetes, cancer, certain autoimmune diseases, and HIV/AIDS. I am not asking teachers to take the place of physicians, but rather to teach about factors that might prevent future illness and the need for annual physical examinations as one ages. If education is to prepare a student for life, let it be a healthy one. This will necessitate education by well-trained and committed teachers who are concerned with both the mind and body.

I have proposed ideas I consider necessary to effect change in our public schools. Some of these suggestions will meet with resistance as they may be difficult to implement. However, there can be little disagreement that our public schools have failed the disadvantaged student of color and the poor particularly. This obligates us, at least, to consider the merit of my proposed changes. If we simply repeat in the future that which we have done in the past, can we really expect different outcomes? As I wrote this book, I realized it would be difficult to achieve the triumph of truth. While opposition can be a useful stimulant, bad faith is a pitiable thing.

The failure of public education for students of color and the underprivileged is, as stated in the introduction, the most significant problem facing our nation. The pain and despair and our neglect is eloquently expressed in the abbreviated passage of *Wind, Sand, and Stars* by Antoine de Saint-Exupéry in the epigraph.

Jonathan Kozol has described this deliberate neglect as "an American apartheid." Our second president, John Adams, wrote, "The education here intended is not merely that of the children of the rich and noble, but of every rank and class of people, down to the lowest and poorest." Albert Einstein cautioned us that without the creative, independently thinking individual, the upward development of society is as unthinkable as the development of the individual without the nourishing soil of the community.[34] There is presently a movement to make certain colleges tuition-free. I hope this happens, but of what benefit is this if many students are not prepared to take advantage of this offer?

I had the privilege of teaching aspects of psychology to family-practice medical residents. I would frequently conclude each lecture with the question "What have you personally done to merit the blessings you have?" Many would respond, they worked hard, owed money, et cetera.

While I acknowledged the truth of their responses, none really answered the question. The message I tried to convey was they actually did very little to merit the blessings they had. I explained they were lucky to have been born to parents who encouraged education and could afford it while sending them to the best possible schools. I encouraged them to never forget when they entered a patient's room what separated them from the patient was luck. In a heartbeat they could just as easily be the one who was in the bed. Is it not the same for the underserved and underprivileged? If we are ever to correct the injustices in our public education, we cannot depend on luck. Parity in schools, improved teaching, and compassionate administrators in innovative programs will minimize the role of biased luck. In our present system it is patently clear that far too many students are unlucky.

We know that truth limps along on the arm of time, but how much longer can we remain indifferent to the poverty, the despair, the helplessness, and violence; the social ills created by the fiction of equal educational opportunity? This indifference, like any festering, untreated wound, will continue to weaken and corrupt our nation. Therefore, equal education for all our citizens is vital because the world as it is makes this goal fundamental for the safekeeping of our civilization. A major revolution in education is long overdue. As the sage Hillel wrote two thousand years ago, "If not now, when?"

APPENDIX: ATTENTION TRAINING MANUAL

TRAINING YOUR STUDENTS to increase their own abilities to attend and concentrate and to improve their memory as well as their ability to self-regulate their own behavior can be accomplished in ten days with only ten minutes of training a day. The acquired skills will help prepare them not just for your class but for the school years that lie ahead.

It is probably better to train children in small groups of seven or eight. If there is a classroom aide, this is usually not a problem since the students will only be separated from the rest of the class for a short period of time. If the class is relatively small, then training can be conducted with the entire group.

Once you have selected your training group, take them to a quiet area and have them lie on blankets, mats, cots, or whatever is available in order to make them comfortable. Explain that the purpose of this training is to help them learn more easily in school. To do this, they will be taught to relax themselves.

Now have them lie on their backs, arms at their sides, and then close their eyes. Tell them to think of their arms growing heavy and warm and relaxing. Repeat this several times, and do not worry about any giggles; that usually stops after a day or two. Repeat the same instructions for their legs.

When the children appear relaxed, instruct them to think of the sun warming their relaxed arms and legs. Now repeat the instructions to relax their arm and legs and to imagine the sun warming their bodies for the remainder of the ten minutes. Shortly, before you end the session and while their eyes are still closed, tell them to relax themselves and lie quietly for about thirty seconds, during which time you, the instructor, will be silent. At the end of thirty seconds instruct the group to open their eyes. The first session is now over.

The instructions for the second and third sessions should be identical to those of the first. The goal is simply to have the children relax and focus on the instructions. Some will do this more than others, but this is not a problem, and never feel that you are inducing a trance-like state. It is simply teaching them to attend to your instructions, and this requires the ability to focus.

At the start of the fourth and fifth sessions during this first week, begin by having the students relax themselves. After observing their behavior, repeat the instructions given the first three sessions simply to reinforce their learning of the technique. Once the students are relaxed have them imagine being in their classroom with other children who are probably talking and even making noise. Encourage them, while relaxed, to ignore the noise and pay attention to the teacher. Scenes descriptive of your classroom can be used during these last two training sessions, the goal being the development of the ability to focus on the teacher's instructions and ignoring other distractions. You, the teacher, are simply teaching the child where and under what conditions he is to focus his attention. The how is intrinsic in the training.

These are general instructions that you, the teacher, really cannot mess up. They are the guidelines that have been proven to work with elementary school students, adults, and even children who have special needs. Trust yourself as you move into the second week of training.

During this second and final week, the students can now be trained as a complete group in their regular classroom while they are sitting in their chairs at desks or tables.

While in their seats, ask them to close their eyes and place their hands on the table and relax themselves. Once they appear relaxed, and you may wish to encourage them to close their eyes, then read aloud a series of numbers. Encourage the group to repeat it immediately after it is read. This is an auditory tracking task. Now repeat this same procedure, **but have the students do it with their eyes open.** Repeat the above using random colors, first with their eyes closed and then with their eyes open.

On the second day of this final training week, again have the students relax in their places. Once they appear to be relaxed, read a sequence of colors to them. Begin with three colors. This time, as a group, they should repeat the series out loud after you present the colors. You might start this auditory retention task first with their eyes closed, then with them open. You then may increase the number of colors to four, five, and even six. There are no fixed rules here, and you are encouraged to adjust this task according to the performance you observe.

During this training session, with eyes still open, they should be asked to repeat complete sentences, such as "The red fox jumped over the blue stick." After they respond, ask them questions such as "What color was the stick?" Make up as many of these task sentences with follow-up questions as you feel the class is enjoying.

During the third and fourth day of this week, give them writing materials, and once relaxed, they are to write down as quickly as possible those numbers, letters, lines, circles—whatever their motor development permits at their respective ages. For example, you might say, "A, four, E," and once you have finished, they should write *A*, 4, *E*. Again, if they are not able to write these letters and numbers, feel free to use circles, lines, et cetera.

On the last day of training, have the students return to where they were trained during the first week. This time, without instruction, just ask them to relax themselves. By now the ability to attend and concentrate has been reinforced as a self-imposed internal set, and the students should be able to use it within their regular classrooms.

Examples of Classroom Applications

Perhaps a child is more active than you feel he or she should be. To help the student regulate their own behavior, please say, "You know what to do, relax yourself." The child should now have the behavioral self-controls. The more you use the expression "you know what to do" during the second week of training, the more strongly you will have established a conditioned cue for the student to bring about the attentional state and voluntary self-control without any need to lecture or admonish.

If you are to begin a group activity or lesson, first say to the entire group, "You know what to do." Initially, after training in this situation, you may add, "Take a little time to relax," and then begin your lesson. With this approach, the group's attention is now focused and receptive to your input.

If any student has, for example, difficulty with a perceptual motor task, please encourage this individual to relax and focus his or her attention before each sequenced step of the task. Parents should also be involved with this technique in order to help their child with homework or in the remediation of lags in educational achievement. We all are aware that each child is unique, not only in their personalities, but in their rates of development and their abilities to achieve all that is expected of them at a particular grade. What will help them is the ability to focus their attention and concentration to facilitate their pace of learning. You, the teacher, are making this goal more likely to happen. You did this when you provided your students with a tool, a technique, to increase their capacity for the self-regulation of their own behavior.

Now, when you say, "You know what to do," or "Relax," the child is more likely to experience personal success in the classroom.

Should the user of this suggested procedure have questions, please contact the author at SHHarlem@icloud.com.

STEVEN HARLEM, P.h.D.

REFERENCES

1. Kozol J. *The Shame of the Nation: The Restoration of Apartheid Schooling in America.* New York: Broadway Books; 2006.
2. Schwartz B, Sharpe K. *Practical Wisdom: The Right Way to Do the Right Thing.* New York: Riverhead Books; 2011:8,29.
3. Dark Ages. Wikipedia. https://en.wikipedia.org/wiki/Dark_Ages_(historiography).
4. Curtis S, Boultwood M. *A Short History of Educational Ideas.* London: University Tutorial Press; 1964:30,53-64.
5. Dewey J. *Democracy and Education.* New York: Macmillan; 1916. https://www.teachthought.com/learning/pedagogy-john-dewey-summary/. Accessed 2011.
6. Tagore R. *Towards Universal Man.* Calcutta, India: Asia Publishing House; 1961.
7. Betsy DeVos and Her No Good, Very Bad Record on Public Education. National Education Association. https://educationvotes.nea.org/2019/03/22/devos/. Published 2019.
8. Radler B. Scientific Imperatives vis-à-vis Growing Inequality in America. *American Psychologist.* 2019;74(7):767.
9. Hancock L. Why Are Finland's Schools Successful? *Smithsonian Magazine.* September 2011. https://www.smithsonianmag.com/innovation/why-are-finlands-schools-successful-49859555/.
10. Carmichael S. America's Education Problem. *Harvard Business Review.* March 15, 2012. https://hbr.org/2012/03/americas-education-problem.
11. Hostinar C, Miller G. Protective factors for youth confronting hardship: Current Challenges and future avenues in resilience research. *American Psychologist.* 2019;74(6):641-652.

12. Porter E. School vs. Society in America's Failing Students. *New York Times*. 2015. https://www.nytimes.com/2015/business/economy/school-vs-society-in-americas-failing-students.html.
13. H. W. Wilson Company. The National Debate Topic: 2017-2018 Education Reform. In: *The Reference Shelf*. Amenia, New York: Grey House Publishing; 2017;89(3):69.
14. Turno G. 10 Major Challenges Facing Public Schools. Public School Review. https://www.publicschoolreview.com/blog/10-major-challenges-facing-public schools.
15. Dynarski M, Kainz K. Why federal spending on disadvantaged students (Title 1) doesn't work. The Brookings Institution. https://www.brookings.edu/research/why-federal-spending-on-disadvantaged students-title-1-doesn't-work/. Published November 20, 2015.
16. Lynch M. Ten Reasons the U.S. Education System Is Failing. Education Week. http://blogs.edweek/education_futures/2015/08/10_reasons_the_education_sysytem_is_failing.html. Published 2015.
17. Murdock S. U.S. Shootings since 1963 Have Killed More Americans than All Wars Ever. *HuffPost*. https://www.huffpost.com/entry/gun-deaths-since-jfk-assassination_n_6e4b016b7d54485c4.
18. Suicide Statistics. American Foundation for Suicide Prevention. https://afsp.org/about-suicide-statistics/. Published 2018.
19. Teenage Pregnancy. United Nations Population Fund. https://en.wikipedia.org/wiki/Teenage_pregnancy.
20. Drug Overdose Deaths. Centers for Disease Control and Prevention. https://www.cdc.gov/durgoverdose/data/statedeaths.html.

21. Buddy T. Alcohol and Drug-Related Crime Statistics. https://www.verywellmind.com/crime-and-alcohol-statistics-from-1998-62821. Updated January 16, 2020.
22. Spending on illicit drugs in US nears $150 billion annually. RAND Corporation. https://www.sciencedaily.com/releases/2019/08/190820081846.htm. Published August 20, 2019.
23. Harlem S. The Effects of Psychophysiological Relaxation upon Selected Learning Tasks in Urban Elementary School Children. *Dissertation Abstracts International.* 1976;36(8).
24. Cubberley E. *Public Education in the United States: A Study and Interpretation of the American Educational History.* Boston: Houghton Mifflin Company; 1919.
25. Raths L, Harmin M, Simon S. *Values and Teaching: Working with Values in the Classroom.* Ohio: Charles E. Merrill Publishing Company; 1966.
26. Ware S. *Forgotten Heroes.* New York: The Free Press; 1998:45–55.
27. Harlem D. Reading Performance of Relaxation Trained Children. *Dissertation Abstracts International.* 1977;38(3).
28. Kids will be Kids, Even in Ancient Rome: Roman Toys & Games. http://www.grandvoyageitaly.com/piazza/kids-will-be-kids-even-in-ancient-rome-toys-games. Published January 27, 2016.
29. Harlem S. Play is Learning. Personal notes. 2008.
30. Patel A. Music and the Brain. Chantilly, Virginia: The Great Courses; 2015.
31. Study Shows Teacher Training Inadequate. https://www.education world.com/a_admin/teacher-prep-inadequate-says-study-shtml.
32. The Normal School. Encyclopedia Britannica. https:www.britannica.com/topic/normal-school.

33. Effects of Fluorescent Lighting on Children's Behavior. Octo Lights. https://www.decorativelightcovers.com/fun-lighting-for-kids-rooms/.
34. Einstein A. Harris A, translator. *The World As I See It*. New York: Citadel Press; 1979:9.

STEVEN HARLEM, P.h.D.

RECOMMENDED READINGS

Harlem S. *The Courage to Think Differently: A Bold Investigation of Prejudice, Human Behavior, and the Power to Revolutionize the Ideas That Shape Our World.* Paper Raven Books, 2019. Available at Amazon.com.

Raths L, Harmin M, Simon S. *Values and Teaching: Working with Values in the Classroom.* Ohio: Charles E. Merrill Publishing Company, 1966. (Out of print, but worth the effort to obtain a used copy).

ACKNOWLEDGMENTS

I am eternally grateful to those many public school students who believed, supported, and accepted me while providing opportunities for me to learn about their lives along with helping me transform my values and express my beliefs. Their faces and stories, if not all their names, are etched in my memory. It is impossible for me to think about our shared adventures without again feeling the associated emotions originally experienced.

I am grateful to Indigo River Publishing for taking a chance on me and guiding me to a wonderful editor, Earl Tillinghast, who held my hand while encouraging me to believe in myself. To Regina Cornell, an extraordinarily talented copyeditor who brings patience and a sensitivity to this author as well as the manuscript, I am eternally thankful for her ability to ripen the fruit of this novice gardener.

A very special and enduring thank-you to Sarah Weinblatt, a generous young woman of superior artistic talent who possesses both rare insight and a compassion well beyond her years.

One undertakes no task in isolation, and I owe a debt of gratitude to M. David, an accomplished writer, whose encouragement was a well I often drank from.

To those few teachers who permitted me to think differently. My one regret is that they are no longer available for me to thank them in person.

At every stage in the writing, I am indebted to my wife, Davida, for her enthusiasm, encouragement, and expression of pride in my efforts.